WORDS AND GESTURES
IN THE LITURGY

Antonio Donghi

WORDS AND GESTURES IN THE LITURGY

Translated from Italian by William McDonough,
Dominic Serra, and Ted Bertagni

A PUEBLO BOOK

Liturgical Press   Collegeville, Minnesota
www.litpress.org

A Pueblo Book published by Liturgical Press

Cover by David Manahan, OSB. Design courtesy of Frank Kacmarcik, OblSB, and *Worship*, May 1992.

An earlier edition of this book was originally published in Italian under the title *GESTI E PAROLE: Un'iniziazione al linguaggio simbolico* (© 1993 by Libreria Editrice Vaticana, 00120 Vatican City) and was published in English under the title *Actions and Words: Symbolic Language and the Liturgy* (© 1997 by Order of Saint Benedict, Collegeville, Minnesota). The current edition is a translation of the revised and expanded Italian edition: *GESTI E PAROLE NELLA LITURGIA: Edizione riveduta e ampliata.* © 2007 by Libreria Editrice Vaticana, 00120 Vatican City. All rights reserved.

Library of Congress Cataloging-in-Publication Data

Donghi, Antonio.
    [Gesti e parole nella liturgia. English]
    Words and gestures in the liturgy / Antonio Donghi ; translated from
Italian by William McDonough, Dominic Serra, and Ted Bertagni.
        p. cm.
    "A Pueblo book."
    ISBN 978-0-8146-6222-9 (pbk.)
    1. Catholic Church—Liturgy.   2. Sacraments—Catholic Church.
3. Christian art and symbolism.   4. Catholic Church—Customs and
practices. 5. Gesture in worship.   6. Gesture—Religious aspects—
Christianity.   I. Title.

BX1970.D6413 2009
264'.02001—dc22   2008054326

Contents

Preface to the Original Edition

The Second Vatican Council's constitution *Dei Verbum* is rightly considered the foundational text of the conciliar teaching. In its first chapter, while presenting the nature and object of revelation, it affirms that this "is realized by deeds and words, which are intrinsically bound up with each other. As a result, the works performed by God in the history of salvation show forth and bear out the doctrine and realities signified by the words; the words, for their part, proclaim the works, and bring to light the mystery they contain" (2).

This is also true for the "dispensation" of salvation that is realized through the liturgical-sacramental economy. Thus the liturgy, a complex of sensible and efficacious signs, is nothing other than the actualization in the present moment of the church of the great works of God in history. Those works have their prelude in the Old Testament and their fullness in Christ, particularly in his paschal mystery (cf. *Sacrosanctum Concilium* 5–7). Thus the possibility—given in our nature as "incarnate spirit"—is opened up to human beings to grasp the invitation and gift of communion with God and all humanity. Through Christ in the Spirit human beings become participants in the mystery of salvation by means of the words and actions that constitute the liturgical celebration. It is the principle of incarnation, or of sacramentality, that controls the whole history of salvation and in which the marvelous condescension of God is revealed. It is also by means of this principle that the wise pedagogy of God wishes to lead us and all people in the fullness of our humanity to a knowledge and experience of the saving event of Easter, that new creation by which the entire human race is being the people of the new covenant.

The words and actions of the divine liturgy, drawn from fundamental and universal human experiences, acquire a fullness of meaning and effectiveness in reference to salvation history, of which the liturgy is a memorial. It follows that participation that is interior as well as active and conscious requires an appropriate initiation into the symbolic language through which the mystery is manifested and made present. Otherwise the celebration of the holy mysteries remains a closed book of seven signs and the ritual action is easily lost in the shallows of ritualism.

This explains why, in the first centuries, the great fathers of the church—both in the East and in the West—gave such attention to mystagogy, which is a process by which believers are progressively led to a knowledge and experience of the Christian mystery. This is a pedagogical work that is indispensable even today. The Italian bishops in their document on the renewal of catechesis put it this way: "The catechist must study and explain the sense, sometimes hidden but always living and inexhaustible, of the liturgical signs and rites. The catechist should observe not so much the natural symbolism of these signs and rites, but more the expressive value they assumed in the history of the old and new covenants. Water, bread, gathering in assembly, walking together in procession, song, and silence all will be able to communicate the truths of salvation that they evoke and mystically effect" (Italian Bishops' Conference, *The Renewal of Catechesis* 115).

The Constitution on the Sacred Liturgy, while speaking of the Eucharist in chapter 2, says that "the Church . . . earnestly desires that Christ's faithful, when present at this mystery of faith, should not be there as strangers or silent spectators." It therefore suggests, in line with the genuine ecclesial tradition, that a liturgical catechesis be done that will guide the faithful to understand that mystery "through a good understanding of the rites and prayers" so that they may participate consciously, fully, and actively (cf. *Sacrosanctum Concilium* 48).

Thirty years after the promulgation of *Sacrosanctum Concilium* it is necessary to recognize that the liturgical reform wished for by Vatican II has not brought forth all the desired fruits of spiritual and pastoral renewal. It is also true that the publication of the new liturgical books and the adoption of new ritual forms have not always been preceded and accompanied by catechesis.

Thus we should be grateful to Fr. Antonio Donghi for this small but precious volume that attempts precisely this catechetical task for pastors and catechists. And we should also be grateful for the simple style and the rich contents that these pages provide the reader. These are characteristics that put Donghi in direct relationship to and logical continuity with Romano Guardini's analogous work *Sacred Signs*

(1930), a work to which the liturgical movement leading to the renewal at Vatican II owes much.

We may hope that a meditative reading of this text will not only facilitate a liturgical catechesis but will also help those who perform the actions of the liturgy and speak its words to do so with competence and interior understanding. This will make for a better manifestation of the paschal mystery of Christ in whom the church lives and on whom it is built up as the body of Christ and a living temple of the Spirit for the sake of the world's salvation.

✢ Luca Brandolini
Auxiliary Bishop of Rome
President of the Episcopal Commission on Liturgy
of the Italian Episcopal Conference

Introduction

The joy of celebrating our faith happens in a multiplicity of verbal and gestural languages to which we do not always pay enough attention. This is true even if we know that the sacramental presence of Christ incarnates itself in sanctifying and meaning-producing signs all along our journey as a believing community (cf. *Sacrosanctum Concilium* 7).

In the diversity and vitality of such signs the church urges us to rejoice as we enter into God's presence and allow ourselves to be wrapped in God's light. Sometimes we are tempted to see our cultural attitudes as external forms, empty of understanding. We run the risk of reading and justifying ritual as a carrier of tradition that we inherit and that we enact simply to fulfill a sacred action while allowing the meaning to slip from our hands. Thus the habit of drama tends to have us celebrate passively the great mysteries of salvation. We should always be alert when we celebrate the liturgy, since to stand in the presence of God, to celebrate the "today" of the Lord, and to allow ourselves to be guided by the Spirit are all ineffable realities for the heart. The incarnation is actualized especially in the liturgy. The richness of the passover of the Lord incarnates itself, communicates itself, and is made personal in every one of us through ritual language.

Every day the Christian community is called to enter into the simplicity of sacramental speech in order to celebrate the gift of the ineffable experience of salvation.

We know that every exterior element of liturgical action has a rapport with an internal vitality that works in the heart of every believer and retranslates itself in diverse actions, making them fruitful so that they may help us grow in the faith. The theological life that animates our spirit is true when it enfleshes itself in love in all its dimensions; every action is a personalization of the one ineffable event of salvation.

We should be attentive each day to learning the various means that God teaches us moment by moment to grasp and express the divine transcendence.

We do not always pay enough attention to the many little acts and behaviors that come our way each day, thereby we lose the profound significance hidden therein. Ordinary life possesses in itself a rich theology: it is not a banal issue for a man or woman to love life as a human being, as a person created in the image and likeness of God.

The human made sick by consumerism and enslaved by the visible, sensate world does not grasp the authentic mysteries that vibrate in his or her inner being. Such a person loses touch with the theology of everyday existence. The liturgy's extraordinary festivity lives and develops from the ordinary when the latter is loved as a gift of God's love. It is within the simple reality of every day, lived with sincerity and purity of heart, that God conceals and reveals the intensity of life that is present in every human creature.

In its language the liturgy loves the things of everyday existence. It puts them at the service of God in obedience to the will of the Lord, so that the human being—who in faith, hope, and love grasps the transcendent—is directed toward God in freedom and joy, finding there a center of gravity. Small things thus become the promise and the premise of greater things, as time is a preparation for eternity.

With the diversity of human languages we are not confronted with something sterile but with the divine richness communicated to us and growing within us by signs.

In the sign of the cross, in the very act of sitting, and in the adoring and genuflecting, we accept the divine invitation to let ourselves be illumined from on high. We talk with God, we give hospitality to the Trinity, and we breathe the divine, who is our very life. Then our action becomes a growing joy and a lively and fruitful profession of faith.

To orient ourselves along this path, we must begin to read the multiple signs that are filled with the word of God. For that word of God animates the liturgy and makes intelligible its very language and the vitality present in the human person. This makes possible a marvelous synthesis of the divine and human.

If we become docile students of the Spirit in understanding the richness of liturgical language, joy will erupt from our spirit, and we will celebrate our faith with expressions that are not merely verbal but that also envelop the whole human being reborn in God. This encourages us to grow in the desire for communion with God in the sacramental encounter experienced through the history of salvation and in our own history.

Surely the liturgy helps us in this growth by means of its repetition and familiar language. Its meanings retranslate themselves over and over and penetrate our whole person as we identify with the Spirit before the face of God.

Our daily reflections give vitality to the liturgy through the celebration of the word, and the depth of its language helps us as a community reach a true spirit of participation in the sacred action and a fruitful expansion of the gift of divine adoption.

Our attention in this book will be given above all to the totality of actions that make up the celebrative experience. Understanding these actions will help us comprehend how limited our language is, but at the same time it will permit us to get a glimpse of the greatness of God, the Ineffable One. It is that One who—in the simplicity of our actions—stands beside us, guides us, builds us up, and helps us grasp the power of the salvation of Christ, our teacher and Lord.

To live the ritual actions becomes a great prayer to God, so that God might become the pastor of a community that with faith moves toward fulfilling the gift of discipleship: the transfiguring contemplation of the Holy Trinity.

The Sign of the Cross

The liturgical celebration always begins with the sign of the cross, which is felt through the entire body of those who are present to celebrate the sacramental presence of Christ.

This ritual gesture comes forth from faith and from a lifestyle that binds together the ordinariness of Christian existence. It is taught from the first moments of baptismal life, and it must define all instances of that life and make our entire journey secure in it. The cross is our great love, since we have been embraced by the glorious Crucified One.

Often we make this sign so much by habit that simply saying the words "In the name of the Father, and of the Son, and of the Holy Spirit. Amen" can lead to a superficiality of heart, and we can easily forget the meaning that is clearly expressed in the movement of our hand.

On the day of our baptism we were immersed in the "image and likeness" of the glorious cross of Christ. That cross has become the heart that beats in our life, the sensibility that animates our choices, the intelligence with which we understand reality, the force that permits us to construct authentic personal relationships, the light that illumines our contact with all created realities. The making of that sign of the cross on our body expresses our desire to grow in relationship with the paschal mystery. Nothing of our human or Christian identity should shrink away from the mystery of the cross.

This truth becomes visible in this sign, which becomes a truly personalized experience. It expresses all the potential that the Spirit has sown in our heart, so that the mystery with which the believing person is surrounded can develop in a sincere and fruitful way. Our whole person comprehends this truth; it sings in everyday life that the death of the Lord has in itself led to the luminosity of the resurrection. The sign made by the hand signifies the light that the Spirit has already impressed on our soul, giving us the new heart promised and dreamed by the prophets.

The word gives meaning to the action. The cross of Jesus lives from the mystery hidden in God in order to recapitulate all things in Christ, "for through him both of us have access in one Spirit to the Father" (Eph 2:18). The cross opens the horizon of our heart to the greatness of trinitarian love and thus illuminates our heart.

The Holy Trinity is the origin of our life; it is the source of human fecundity and the goal of all our history. With the Spirit we enter into communion with the source of life: the Father, the Son, and the Holy Spirit, and in and with them, with all our brothers and sisters, that we may live this communion in unity with one another. As the Teacher has said to us, "And I, when I am lifted up from the earth, will draw all people to myself" (John 12:32).

Our every celebration, filled with the splendor of the cross, is animated with this richness. We begin our celebrations in the power of the paschal mystery so that we might live our communion in the Holy Spirit to the glorification of the Father. The ritual sequences that give shape to the liturgical assemblies live from the spirit of the cross and are the incarnation of it, while they also create unity among the celebrants. We are not able to live that communion unless we have been profoundly immersed in the cross. The truth of the cross manifests itself in the growth of communion in the Christian community.

We express this marvelous synthesis every time we make the sign of the cross, which should give us great cause for reflection. Is the sensibility that animates all moments of our life the hymn of the wisdom of the cross? Are our relationships made fruitful in the death and resurrection of the Teacher?

Often we are tempted to live this communion without the cross, since we may not choose to long for the source of life and its wisdom. The truth of our existence is that tree from which springs the life that is fraternity, union, communion, and communication in that unity for which the Redeemer died and is risen.

The proclamation that Jesus "died according to the Scriptures, was buried and rose on the third day according to the Scriptures" is alive in our spirit and grows with us through the ordinary gesture of the cross, which, because it is ordinary, allows us to understand the deep profundity within it. Such an experience makes us love the cross: we no longer see it as a source of closure, of depression, or of failure but as the way to truly become ourselves. From the cross we see the world with the heart and the eyes of Christ, and we rejoice in that divine intimacy that is the unique source of the meaning of our lives. Parents and godparents, when they trace the sign of the cross on the forehead of the baby at baptism, take on the responsibility of educating it in the very way of the dead and risen Jesus so that the infant's life may be a continuing expression of Jesus' way. This is what the baptismal ritual tells us at the moment of the initial signing with the cross. To trace "on the baby the sign of Christ the Savior" means to help the baby learn "to love God and neighbor as Christ has taught us." Thus we see that the sign of the cross is the beginning of true life, that it is the meaning of our own ascension toward the fullness of glory, and that it is the expression of our self-identification in the paschal mystery that we will live in the heavenly Jerusalem. There we will follow the Lamb wherever he may go so that we may be washed in his blood.

The Gathering

On the day of our baptism we were introduced into the Christian community that welcomed us as a gift of the Holy Spirit. Slowly growing in divine life and in the experience of communion, we began learning the joy of being "us." The Christian is a "communitarian" person, who lives in the image of the Holy Trinity: he or she no longer lives alone, since whoever is in Christ is a member of the communion, even when physically distant. Our spirit trembles with a continual longing for communion, because it knows the urgency of incarnating the gift of divine life in our daily situations and of making all our brothers and sisters participants in that life.

When we gather in the "sacred space" we live the life of those united in the name of the Lord, because we have been converted by hearing the word that introduced us to the evangelical way of life, to the hope that lives from the ineffable action of the Holy Spirit, and to the vitality of the love that the Father has infused in our hearts.

Our assemblies breathe the divine, since the Spirit lingers therein and since Christ acts at the center of our assemblies for the glory of the Father.

How difficult it is for the contemporary person to rediscover the meaning of the gift of faith, to be part of an ideal community, to participate with others as sisters and brothers!

When we gather we are not persons who freely and on our own initiative decide to come together. We are the called, the elect, the loved. In Christ the Father has chosen us from the creation of the world to find ourselves in God's presence, holy and spotless in love (Eph 1:4), so that we may develop the true sense of communion (see Col 3:12-17). Only the continual rediscovery of the centrality of Christ will help us understand this context.

Christ has snatched us from our loneliness—made of marginalizations and frustrations—and from the sin that makes us slaves of our ego, of our emotions, and of the insecurities of the "flesh." All these enclose us within our brief and limiting horizon. Yet Christ has also introduced us into communion with the Father, Son, and Holy Spirit, with all the brothers and sisters we encounter on our way, and with all human beings who breathe in the creative power of God.

The liturgy invites us to rediscover our human vocation—to grow in communion, to be the people of God, to work with and for our brothers and sisters in the dynamic of celebration.

The liturgy helps us become aware that our existence is true if it knows how to sing the "we" of the Holy Trinity. The liturgical assembly helps us bring to life once again the joy and abundance of the apostolic church (cf. Acts 2:42-47). The gnawing doubt that stands to ruin our ritual gathering is mindful of those immediate goals that distance us from the Gospel. For the Gospel gradually changes the heart of the person, introducing it into that divine experience of communion that will be full when God will be all in all.

Our hearts should be open to the strong requests and demands that lead us to live the gift of union with our brothers and sisters. The spirit of our assemblies depends on what passes into our hearts from the questions that influence us, from the lights that guide us in dialogue toward living the sign of together rediscovering how God is in our hearts in communion with the Holy Trinity.

If the liturgy educates us for the rediscovery of this divine project, our gathering together in cultic assembly should ask us about our way of living with our brothers and sisters in everyday life. As a consequence, the thirst for communion, which rises in the human heart and tends to find illusory solutions within history, finds in the genuine celebration of the liturgical communion the place where our thirst is sated.

We are the sign of the church, of the truth of divine thought, when we gather in the name of the Lord and are called to give witness to his Spirit, to his word, to his death and resurrection, and to his mission. The joy of the assembly is a passivity that generates an inexhaustible activity. Called together by the Spirit, we love in the manner of Pentecost. Called around the one altar, we become one body and one soul, just as the epiclesis in the eucharistic prayer teaches us.

The time in which we live the gift of the assembly is the "today" of our salvation, of our passage from Babel to Pentecost, from sin to grace. The unity that animates the assembly signifies that humanity ought to gather in the temple of God as the sign of God's presence growing and expanding with us in his unity as we journey through life. To allow ourselves to be educated by such a mystery of communion demands that we be receptive to the Holy Spirit, who calls us to a conversion that draws us away from our isolation and allows us to grow in our longing to drink from the one fountain of life: the paschal mystery.

The joy of our gathering is that in contemplating the Crucified One our assembly may become "the cross of Christ" in which we live and move and act.

The vitality of our gathering in the name of the Lord will take on new meaning by becoming a prophetic sign for a world looking for the true unity in which it can find true peace.

When we walk in truth we reflect the presence of the Holy Spirit, who gathers us to Christ and introduces us to the divine newness. We know that our gathering in the name of the Lord is a sacrament, a passing and provisional sign that must one day give way to the great and universal convocation dreamed of by the prophets (cf. Isa 25:6ff.) and lived by Christ (cf. John 11:52) in an unreserved longing for the heavenly Jerusalem, when all people will be fully saved because they will be fully configured with Christ. May this be our hope. Our assemblies must never be closed in on themselves in petty and narrow ways according to the "flesh." May they always breathe that longing for growth in communion that transcends race, nation, and language so that we all might enter that gifted state of being gathered in the sacrament of full and glorious communion, singing as one the new hymn presented by the saints to God and to the Lamb.

Standing Together

The *General Instruction of the Roman Missal* affirms: "A common posture, to be observed by all participants, is a sign of the unity of the members of the Christian community gathered for the sacred Liturgy: it both expresses and fosters the intention and spiritual attitude of the participants. . . . The faithful should stand from the beginning of the Entrance chant or while the priest approaches the altar, until the end of the collect; for the *Alleluia* chant before the Gospel; while the Gospel itself is proclaimed; during the Profession of Faith and the Prayer of the Faithful; from the invitation, *Orate, fratres* (*Pray, brethren*), before the prayer over the offerings until the end of the Mass, except at the places indicated below" (42–43).

These instructions flow from the spiritual experience that animates the faithful during the liturgy. The joy of our togetherness in the assembly expresses itself in our standing together: this common posture of the body underlies a whole range of feelings and interior convictions that resound when the soul stands in the presence of God and has a sense of being in a living dialogue with the divine.

We remain standing because we are before the one who determines and defines our life, who gives strength to our existence and makes it full. Before God, we stand up, coming to our feet in order to say that God is the only Lord. This is as the Scriptures teach us in the meeting of Abraham with God at the oak of Mamre (Gen 18:8). We stand out of respect to the Most High.

Even when caught up in many cares and human projects, our existence is always before God, for we say with our life that there is no purpose greater than God's love. For this reason our prayer expresses itself in our standing together, as the assembly of Israel did while King Solomon dedicated the temple to God and recited his long prayer (cf. 1 Kgs 8:14). The divine is recognized as the force that gives life to the human person; the standing person gives witness to the gratitude and the familiarity he or she has with God.

The standing assembly expresses the living relationship by which it is united to God, and it exhibits that the people are aware that their lives are an upward course toward the fullness of communion with God in glory.

The history of religions teaches us about this ritual posture. The ancients constructed their temples on hills in order to indicate visibly a greater closeness to God. In like manner, the very posture of standing at prayer tends to place one in a more intensive communion with the divine and expresses clearly being closer to the Most High. Such an attitude, or posture, becomes particularly significant in the moments of the proclamation of the faith—both in the Creed and in the eucharistic prayer—since with this gesture we proclaim before the world that the truth that comes from on high and illumines our spirit unites us in an intimate communion with Christ. We profess publicly that the Lord's passover is the foundation of our existence in all of its manifestations.

The death and resurrection of Jesus constitute the defining nucleus of our life; thus every time this truth resounds in our assemblies we cannot keep from springing to our feet to express our deep gratitude.

The Gospel that represents the living announcement of this truth is the foundation of our life. The paschal event, perceived in our constant and active attention to the mystery, resounds in our whole way of being and acting.

Just as the death of the Lord defines us, the faithfulness of the Father is the font of our spirit's joy. Standing together as we profess our faith reveals the joy our heart feels when it proclaims the resurrection of the Lord. Such rejoicing infuses into the believing person an understanding and certainty of his full being. A faith that was not proclaimed in the joy of the heart would not be able to emerge in all its existential power. Standing together is a gestural proclamation.

The paschal message is operative in this standing together and puts us in a living and fruitful posture of sharing the death and resurrection of the Lord, a living way of placing ourselves in an exodus pilgrimage. The joy of the resurrection leads us toward the Spirit and makes us fully aware of the faithfulness of the Father. We can walk in a newness of life all the way to the mountain of God, where we will live in eternal contemplation of the glory of the Father. We listen while standing in order to accept the word, in order to be attentive to the truths of life given by the Master. We can decisively, radically, and irreversibly abandon any habits that block us from a full pilgrimage leading us to the eternal pastures of the kingdom. Standing together with Jesus, we climb toward Jerusalem, since at the foot of the cross we are able to partake in his glorification. The assembly is not static and motionless during the celebration; rather, it is in constant movement toward participation in the paschal victory of the Master in the heavenly Jerusalem.

He who is standing is ready to accomplish that which the Spirit tells the church, to be able then to participate in the paschal victory of the Teacher in the eternal Jerusalem.

Our standing together thus helps us refrain from pretending that we can find in ourselves the criteria by which we can live. Rather, this standing is an act of praying faith that proclaims to the world that salvation comes from on high: "I lift up my eyes to the hills—/ from where will my help come? / My help comes from the LORD,/ who made heaven and earth" (Ps 121:1-2).

Thus our spiritual life gives vitality to the language of the liturgy. Not content to accept the contingent reality, but attentive and vigilant—as the sentinel who waits in the morning for the sun to rise—in order to proclaim the good news of salvation and redemption.

The liturgy's invitation to stand together expresses the joy of our believing heart that longs to grow to the full stature of Jesus Christ, dead and risen. It invites us to join in a fruitful pilgrimage through the desert of life and to proclaim our faith in his passover.

4

Kneeling Together

The Christian tradition constantly recalls us to the practice of kneeling. The kneelers present in our churches constitute in themselves an invitation for us to kneel, above all, for personal prayer. Such a posture disposes us to a variety of interior attitudes, inspiring the heart and helping to overcome any temptation of self-sufficiency, common enough for people who feel the need always to stand on their own two feet and for whom kneeling could suggest failure. What emerges immediately in kneeling is a sense of being in the presence of the Lord, as the psalm says: "O come, let us worship and bow down, / let us kneel before the LORD, our Maker! / For he is our God, / and we are the people of his pasture, / and the sheep of his hand" (Ps 95:6-7). Before the Ineffable we can do nothing else but fall on our knees and proclaim, even by physical posture, that God is the Lord of life. Such a posture underlines the spirit of humility that penetrates and animates our heart.

Often we say that we are in the presence of God and that we are mindful of the lordship of the Spirit. Such affirmations should not merely be nice expressions that do not reflect our inmost thoughts. We must always remember that such interior attitudes should result in kneeling, the posture where a believer reaches truth. Such a gesture is a concrete sign of a heart that adores. The rejoicing of our spirit brings to life the posture of the elders in the book of Revelation as they prostrate themselves before the Lamb (cf. 5:8-14). A person intuits divine power and sings its wonders while prostrate on the earth, proclaiming with the whole self the greatness of the Lord.

This posture brings us to a profound spirit of adoration, in which God's plan is revealed. It is an instruction offered to us by the liturgy of the solemnity of Christmas, in which we are called to kneel while professing our faith in the gift of the incarnate Word ("by the power of the Holy Spirit / he was born of the Virgin Mary, and became man"), and by the adoration of the cross in the afternoon celebration of Good Friday ("This is the wood of the cross, on which hung the Savior of the world. / Come, let us worship").

The assembly that falls on its knees relives the affirmation of Jesus: "I thank you, Father, Lord of heaven and earth, because you have hidden these things from the wise and the intelligent and have revealed them to infants" (Matt 11:25). It is a welcoming of the God who descends, overtaking all those who celebrate and expand their desire to walk in truth, in love, and in justice. Falling to our knees, we bring to life the prayer present in our spirit, so that the Lord might define us and breathe life into our intention, and come to live in our very being and infuse our members with the energy of total obedience and self-offering into the Father's hands. The divine light is indispensable for our spirit, since we live, breathe, and act in it. "Your word, O Lord, is a lamp for our steps," Psalm 119 repeats to us unceasingly. Our kneeling is an expression of the heart that opens itself before the divine in order to experience communion with the Most High.

Kneeling in order to give hospitality to the truth that comes from on high teaches us the sense of our own poverty as creatures and of our weakness as sinners. When we kneel we express our desire to be in harmony with Christ, and at the same time we point to the strong dissonance between such a gift and our own concrete existence. In the face of the real unfolding of the Father's plan we kneel in order to admit the heaviness of our spirit, which does not succeed in translating into the ordinariness of life that which the Father wants of us. Still, such a posture of meekness and humility is also the expression of our deeply rooted conviction that he who has begun his work in us will bring it to fulfillment.

Our kneeling thus becomes the simple acceptance of the divine plan in full certainty that God in the Spirit will fill the poverty of our ordinariness. This is the posture of the *ordinandi* at the moment of the prayer of ordination. They kneel so that the Spirit, lingering on their persons, will infuse in them the divine power that works the paschal mysteries, to the glory of the Father and to the salvation of all humanity. In that kneeling on the day of ordination the presbyter is clothed in the vestment of his ministerial fruitfulness.

In sum, our kneeling represents the exercise of a profound recognition of our sin. We too, like the publican in the Gospel of Luke (18:13), kneel down as penitents and say, "God, be merciful to me, a sinner!" We recognize that only the divine power can raise us up from our failure and distance from God. It is the posture we assume when in the sacrament of penance we acknowledge our sin in the living certainty that the power of the paschal mystery will raise us up and return us to a faithful following of the path presented by the Lord's passover.

This truth can be understood because, according to the tradition, the faithful were not to kneel during the season of Easter: they were to celebrate the joy of the resurrection. Only after Pentecost did the penitents once again kneel.

Every time we fall to our knees, we live the evangelical affirmation: "Whoever humbles himself will be exalted." We should always rejoice in the Holy Spirit when in truth of heart we kneel. On the one hand we acknowledge our humble condition in the face of the Ineffable, and on the other we underline our complete openness to the divine action that lifts up the humble and unfolds in their hearts the power of God's revelation.

5

Genuflecting

When we enter church, our most common and spontaneous gesture before the tabernacle and the solemnly exposed Blessed Sacrament is that of genuflecting. With this gesture every Christian who comes into such a place of worship makes an act of faith, signifying the ritual and communal vitality of the liturgical celebration. It is an expansion of the profession of faith in Christ dead and risen.

In the *General Instruction on the Roman Missal* the following appears: "During Mass, three genuflections are made by the priest celebrant: namely, after the showing of the host, after the showing of the chalice, and before Communion. . . . If, however, the tabernacle with the Most Blessed Sacrament is present in the sanctuary, the priest, the deacon, and the other ministers genuflect when they approach the altar and when they depart from it, but not during the celebration of Mass itself. Otherwise all who pass before the Most Blessed Sacrament genuflect, unless they are moving in procession" (274). Such genuflections help us understand the eucharistic event and serve as an expression of the paschal mystery.

Genuflecting is not merely a simple ritual moment but a retracing of the will to live the paschal mystery even in individual piety. It expresses a profound spirit of adoration present and active in the believer and underlines the lordship of God in one's life. This is what the apostle Paul teaches us in the letter to the Philippians: ". . . so that at the name of Jesus / every knee should bend, / in heaven and on earth and under the earth, / and every tongue should confess / that Jesus Christ is Lord, / to the glory of God the Father" (2:10-11).

Genuflecting is a sign of the life-giving confession of faith in the paschal mystery, and it is a manifestation of the believing will that longs to participate in the mystery of the death and resurrection of the Lord.

The eucharistic mystery, constituting the center of the life of the Christian community, celebrates our whole being, since in faith and in baptism we have been called to die and to rise constantly as a participation in the sacrificial banquet of the paschal mystery by sharing fully the sentiments of the Redeemer. It is Paul who teaches us: "We do not live to ourselves, and we do not die to ourselves. If we live, we live to the Lord, and if we die, we die to the Lord; so then, whether we live or whether we die, we are the Lord's" (Rom 14:7-8).

Our bending of the knee is a gesture of profound faith, since it is a lived profession of the revealed truth that "Christ died for our sins in accordance with the scriptures, and that he was buried, and that he was raised on the third day in accordance with the scriptures" (1 Cor 15:3-4). Genuflecting in itself is particularly significant. While bending our knee to the ground is our acknowledgment of our vocation to participate in and to grow in the likeness of the death of the Lord, it is also our hope to rejoice in the vitality of the resurrection, which we recall as we get up from the ground.

The lowering of ourselves in the presence of the cross of Christ, as the liturgy of Good Friday asks of us, or in the presence of the Eucharist during and after sacramental celebrations, expresses a readiness to commend ourselves as an offering to the Father. We do this in imitation of the suffering of Jesus on the cross in order that we may also experience the richness of the resurrection.

The repetition of this gesture of faith leads the community to an always fuller personalization of the paschal mystery. Having been saved, we must walk in a newness of life (cf. Rom 6:4), living the humbleness of the Savior (cf. Phil 2:6-11).

The act of genuflecting teaches us daily to live as did Christ. It leads us to enter into his holy and living offering and sacrifice and to recognize that there is no other name by which humanity can be saved.

When we enter into a full openness toward the Father, bending our knee in submission to his wishes, we live in the certainty that God is faithful, that God never disappoints. In fact, we abandon all our self-sufficiency in order to recognize that only the Father of our Lord Jesus Christ is the Lord of our lives. In genuflecting we make the abandonment of the psalmist our own: "The LORD is my chosen portion and my cup; / you hold my lot" (Ps 16:5).

Unfortunately, the routine nature of this gesture, which we repeat frequently in celebrations and in personal devotion, becomes such a habit that it does not always have all the internal meaning that we might desire, and it does not lead us to make of our life a profession of faith for the world to see. In this gesture we should want to show our full commitment to the glorious Christ who carries in himself the signs of the cross and of death. We should say to the world that "We should glory in the cross of our Lord Jesus Christ, for he is our salvation, our life and our resurrection; through him we are saved and made free" (entrance antiphon, evening Mass of the Lord's Supper on Holy Thursday).

Our genuflecting is an active living of our faith. It is a making conscious what it means to believe. It is a letting oneself be led to construct one's own life in profound humility before the Father in imitation of the Redeemer. Then, our every instant may be as a dying of the "old self," who does not know how to discern according to the Spirit, so that we may allow ourselves to be invaded by the light that comes from on high and becomes the resurrection. Thus the person lives every fragment of time not depending of the fidelity of human beings, but essentially counting on the divine fidelity that is never lacking to give meaning to our imperturbable desires. Our own ascending toward the Father makes the mystery of the death and resurrection of Christ alive in a compelling manner. Genuflecting recalls this life with Christ to us, reminding us of the necessity of a daily paschal conversion.

The conclusion of this spiritual journey will be our full configuration to the Master in the liturgy of the saints in the heavenly Jerusalem.

Being Seated

The room in which the liturgical assembly gathers always includes seating that serves a useful function in the liturgy. The Sacramentary indicates that the people should "sit while the readings before the Gospel and the responsorial Psalm are proclaimed, and for the homily and while the Preparation of the Gifts at the Offertory is taking place; and as circumstances allow, they may sit or kneel while the period of sacred silence after Communion is observed" (*General Instruction on the Roman Missal* 43). Such a posture in itself has a biblical resonance. When the word is proclaimed during the celebration, the people are similar to the disciples who listened to the words of the Master in the Sermon on the Mount (cf. Matt 5:1) or to Mary who delighted in listening to Jesus while seated at his feet and who received his praise: "Mary has chosen the better part, which will not be taken away from her" (Luke 10:42).

The gesture of being seated has a wide range of meanings. The posture of the seated body suggests an expectation of something; it facilitates hearing and the reception of a message from wherever it may come. It supports attention, meditation, and spiritual contemplation. The sense of rest assumed by the body suggests a similar disposition of the person.

Being seated also suggests particular mental situations. It expresses a profound will to discover the true significance of life. The Christian seeks that significance in God. In the gesture of being seated the person indicates visibly the intimate desire that God would speak, that God would give the person values by which to live. This being seated is an epiclesis in action, that God might come and be revealed.

Also, in being seated a profound sense of quiet and repose flourishes that permits a person to welcome God's word. While seated a person is fully attentive, open, and in the most favorable posture for receiving instruction in the faith.

In fact, with this gesture the assembly says that God is Lord and asks that the divine light penetrate our hearts. The physical relaxation peculiar to being seated says that one's spirit does not want to be defensive before the divine will. God desires to reside within the human person, to make that person fruitful and to permeate all his or her sensibilities.

This posture then translates itself into an inner decision to share the word of life, to communicate the interior experience in order to enrich the community, to encourage this shared spiritual sensibility in others. Being seated expresses an ardent desire for communion. Jesus is the master in this. In the Johannine narration of Jesus' meeting with the Samaritan woman, we are told: "Jesus, tired out by his journey, was sitting by the well" (John 4:6). Here Jesus is seated as he communicates truth; that action expresses an anxiousness for truth. It brings an interior serenity to the heart of the woman who comes to meet him. In fact, the heart, when it is filled with great things and rejoices in them, sees the urgency of being seated with its brothers and sisters in order to make them participants in the gift that has been received. To find ourselves together to share the word is very enriching. This can happen through Scripture sharing sessions, with a related growth in Christian sensibility, or in dialogue homilies. In such a way every baptized person exercises his or her own priesthood, becoming the voice of the Spirit for the community, and the community members share the unique gift that the Spirit has offered to every one of them.

Such a posture sheds light on the prophetic dimension of the Christian community and proclaims to the world that the daily bread of the saved is the word, which feeds their life and makes them experience the joy of the salvation that comes from on high.

The sense of tranquility in the act of being seated represents well the eschatological rest, as the author of Revelation introduces us to the contemplation of the eternal communion: "To the one who conquers I will give a place with me on my throne, just as I myself conquered and sat down with my Father on his throne" (Rev 3:21).

The movement to be seated, while it underlines the joy of wanting to rest, orients one toward eternal communion in God. It evidences a profound aspiration for the homeland in which the creature will find the definitive place of true and perfect life. In the act of being seated a desire flowers for eternal vision; we show that to the word heard in the liturgical assembly there will come one day a fullness of joy. Our spirit will be penetrated by the divine communication, and in the eternal light will rejoice in being fully itself. Being seated allows the ineffable communication of the Eternal to happen, that full communication between the transfiguring gaze of God and every person in eternity.

If being seated allows this profound communication, such a richness will be totally realized in the heavenly Jerusalem. In the liturgy of heaven we will experience these feelings and these states of the spirit in a singular way. We will be in eternal quiet, in the full silence of recollection, in the intimate and beatifying possession of the reality that does not die. In the divine luminosity we will be freed from anxiety and from the preoccupation of losing fleeting moments of relational joy, preoccupations we frequently face in our life's journey. For we are always aware of the limits of our dialogue, of being seated in view of a parting. Because this is true, we are distanced from the joy of our encounter. This present reality will be definitively overcome when we seat ourselves eternally at the banquet of the kingdom.

This experience may be truly exalting for our spirit. Every time we are seated, our spirit enters into that peace that helps us receive the divine word and taste the progressive communication with God.

When we enter a church and are seated, we spontaneously notice the sensation of living that peace that comes from the word of the one through whom we are enriched. We have a foretaste of the eternal joy that awaits us, and we are moved to live with other human beings, our brothers and sisters, to share with them the joy of the divine peace that should animate every one of our relationships and should help us grow together in our one hope.

Being Silent

One particular aspect underlined in the conciliar reform is that of sacred silence (cf. *Sacrosanctum Concilium* 30). In the *General Instruction for the Liturgy of the Hours*, we find this statement: "In order to receive in our hearts the full sound of the voice of the Holy Spirit and to unite our personal prayer more closely with the word of God and the public voice of the Church, it is permissible, as occasion offers and prudence suggests, to have an interval of silence. . . . Care must be taken to avoid the kind of silence that would disturb the structure of the office, or annoy and weary those taking part" (202).

The Byzantine liturgy recalls this attitude of silence in a very solemn way so that the proclamation of the Gospel may be heard: "Wisdom, be attentive! Let us hear the holy Gospel," and the Roman liturgy explicitly requests silence after the invitation of the celebrant, "Let us pray." Such indications of the magisterial teaching and of liturgical practice help us understand the importance that silence should have in the dynamic of the liturgical celebration.

To be silent is never to lead to that emptiness that a person feels when being forced to be silent. Being silent reveals particular attitudes that arise from an interior richness: the living consciousness of finding oneself in the presence of God who reveals his face and salvation to us. The person, when placed before the Creator, glorifies God above all by means of silence, in conformity to what the ancients have said: God is honored with silence, because silence is praise of the Most High. To be silent is to recognize ourselves as needy creatures in the presence of the divine. Silence also allows the intensity of the human heart's pleading for God to come.

This interior attitude responds to the call that God addresses to the person in order for that person to express an authentic openness to revelation. In fact, this silence is the normal environment in which communion with God is lived and developed. Its function is to place us in the divine communion so that God's face can be manifested to us. God lives this silence, since God's interior vitality is silence. Our own being silent underlines the urgency of our heart to contemplate God's ineffable luminosity.

Silence is never empty, a useless time that should be filled. Instead, it is the realm of divine abundance. It is the epiclesis of the believing soul that longs for the Absolute. It is the ritual and existential attitude before any true and determining encounter with God. When we are silent, we live again the experience of Nazareth. We rejoice in the incarnation, and we taste the "now" of God who saves us.

Such an interior richness demands that we know how to rediscover the profound sense of silence that accompanies every season of one's life. When God leads us to silence, God invites us to take a qualitative jump in the construction of our life, to penetrate the profundity of existence, and to grasp that which is essential in making every instant of our life's pilgrimage rich. To be silent thus generates a living thirst for the word.

Waiting generates silence. It is the attitude of the hearers of Jesus in the synagogue of Nazareth: "And he rolled up the scroll, gave it back to the attendant, and sat down. The eyes of all in the synagogue were fixed on him" (Luke 4:20).

The Most High generates silences in the mystery of love and increases the thirst that only God's own coming can fill. When we achieve true silence, we affirm that our spirit has been conquered by God. Thus our life is a reflection of the divine indwelling in our heart.

Silence is a living openness of the human heart toward the Infinite. It is a pulling down of every defense in the face of God's self-manifestation. It is a taking pleasure in the divine liberty within the human spirit. It is the joy of giving hospitality to the Giver of every gift. Silence thus shows the soul's urgency for communion with God.

Often we act as if the best language for interpersonal communion were words and dialogue. Yet if we penetrate into the world of God, we notice that silence constitutes the habitual language of the relation-ship among Father, Son, and Holy Spirit. The person who lives with silence accepts the other beyond any differences, and the other rejoices in being accepted as a gift. Silence thus becomes the active expression of the living consciousness of dialogue.

All the expressions that arise in the liturgy are born from the ineffable silence of the communion that exists between God and the community and between the Spirit and the soul. These expressions become the occasion for a spiritual and existential deepening until the day when that soul will enter into full communion with the Holy Trinity. It is the posture of Mary listening in front of Jesus, and it prefigures the posture of disciples in the heavenly Jerusalem.

Our silence is an expression of joy. The intensity that silence brings of rapport with others and with God arises from the rejoicing of every Christian that his or her soul is wrapped up in and permeated by the divine. Only a superficial person sees the moment as something passing and of no interest. The truth of every encounter is the abundance of the silence of the soul. The person who is distracted and weary with rushing allows everything to pass and lives an inconsistent life.

Silence becomes the place of deepening, of meditation, of discernment of the word, of personalizing the encounter with God, sounding the depths and the infinite richness of divine manifestation. Silence allows the movement toward full communion with the Absolute to emerge.

Silence lives in one's heart after the celebration of the Eucharist, the Liturgy of the Hours, and after every sacrament and moment of intense personal prayer. We notice the coming of the divine as we acquire a deepened taste of eternal joy—until we can see the one whom we may now only taste sacramentally and in the revelation in the word.

To be silent marks the greatness of the human being, who rejoices in the gift of life and who accepts God who never ceases to meet the one who searches. In silence we notice the anxiousness of waiting, an anxiousness that makes us rejoice in the Spirit and sing the joy of divine communion, as we see the sense of our own life and that of the whole Christian community.

8

Proclaiming

Upon reaching the ambo in the liturgical celebration, the lector proclaims the Sacred Scriptures to the assembly. This act acquires its vitality from the history of salvation expressed in the Old Testament. The term "to proclaim" expresses the interior attitude of the one who is called by the Spirit to be herald of the Anointed One, the One expected by all humanity, and the source of every joy that fills the heart of every creature.

The context of the celebration does not allow us to use terms like "to read" or "to say," thus limiting the message to be communicated as if it were mere information. The word is proclaimed, because it is God who makes an appeal to the human heart, calling it to a full conversion. A sense of being a conveyor of the word moves the one who reads to adopt a proper internal disposition, rendering the communication of the word incisive in every hearing.

To proclaim the Scriptures is to cry out to the world a sense of life; the fullness already operating in the heart of the lector overflows. This cry arises from the soul of the one who is enamored by truth, who senses that truth is central to every brother and sister of every community. The act of crying out illumines every human being who is in search of truth.

The tone of voice reveals a profound conviction of life that comes alive in the herald, a joyful promise that, long awaited, now has fulfillment. A great apostolic anxiousness is proper for the one who would bring the Gospel of hope to the world. Yet it also shows that humanity truly stands waiting for the word that can give people a turning point, giving strength to those who entrust themselves to that word and showing a way to reach fullness of life.

The liturgical proclamation of the word allows us to relive the announcement of salvation, just as the prophet Isaiah describes it: "How beautiful upon the mountains / are the feet of the messenger who announces peace, / who brings good news, / who announces salvation, / who says to Zion, 'Your God reigns'" (52:7).

The anxiousness of the prophets who cry out the word of the Most High in order to call the people to conversion is incarnate in every lector who announces the "today" of paschal salvation in the liturgical celebration. Proclaiming the Gospel becomes a divine communication by means of the human voice and introduces the assembly to an experience of faith. The disciple of the Lord does not "say" her or his faith, since in such a moment the lector is not formulating principles, is not presenting an argument, is not delicately convincing the other. Rather, with voice and spirit the lector cries out the content of the faith, as did the apostle Paul: "every tongue should confess / that Jesus Christ is Lord, / to the glory of God the Father" (Phil 2:11). The disciple communicates to all present the mighty works of the Father in the paschal gift (cf. Acts 2:11). God speaks in order to awaken the human heart and to prevent it from being "choked by the cares and riches and pleasures of life" (Luke 8:14).

This crying out and proclaiming the Gospel calls for a fullness of faith in the one proclaiming, respect for the Most High, and a unity of heart and voice that makes the proclaimer an authentic prophet of salvation and conversion.

Only the one who is rooted in faith and pervaded by the message of the Gospel is clothed with force and joy, and thus "cries out." Such a person is a living sign of the salvation of all humanity. Life experienced simply as a passage of time can generate profound apathy in our hearts and a tragic monotony produced by the mere multiplication of life's isolated moments. Thus a person can be in danger of being weighed down by life's "non-sense" and of being lulled into a spiritual slumber. The believer, however, proclaims to the world the exuberance of faith, so that every human being might grow in hope and find again the will to live. In this "crying out" there is the good news of life. It is the cry of the prophet Isaiah to the disheartened: "The Lord GOD has given me the tongue of a teacher, / that I may know how to sustain the weary with a word" (50:4). It is the great apostolic attestation of Peter and John before the Sanhedrin: "Whether it is right in God's sight to listen to you rather than to God, you must judge; for we cannot keep from speaking about what we have seen and heard" (Acts 4:19-20).

The gesture of proclaiming the Scriptures during the liturgy retranslates just such a foundational conviction. The proclaiming by the lector should be a translation of the divine richness that generates hope, joy, faith, and light in whoever is truly listening.

"The congregation proclaims their praise" (Sir 44:15). Salvific force reaches the assembly joined by the power of the Holy Spirit and animated by the light of the Gospel. The believing community is regenerated by the crying out of hope that comes from the proclamation of the word. It is reanimated and takes joy in being in the place of a living gift of grace, since in the proclamation of salvation God's faithfulness is renewed. In the assembly, then, the joy of Easter morning lives and the climate of Pentecost breathes again. The crying out of the faithful is an expression of the joy that overtakes them and grounds them in the certainty that God accompanies them.

The common proclamation of faith is the prophetic crying out to the whole world that it should awaken to the voice of the Lord, that it should search for the truth and long to be joined with the one Word of life: Jesus Christ.

By means of the prophet's crying out, God speaks and gives hope to humanity. Also, by proclaiming together the wonders of God, as in the process of osmosis, every person will infect every member of the community with an experience of communion and hope.

Proclaiming the great works of God makes us realize that we are a saved people, but a people who continually need to be saved and who possess the certainty that there will always be a place for salvation with God. It is to cry out to the world that even today God is faithful in Jesus Christ.

9

Listening

The celebrant, initiating the Liturgy of the Word at the Easter Vigil, addresses the faithful: "Dear friends in Christ, we have begun our solemn vigil. Let us now listen attentively to the word of God." What the vigil celebration puts in clear light is also the scene of every liturgical action, in which one is called by the very posture of listening to find oneself as a human being.

In fact, listening is the fundamental posture of the disciple of the Lord, whose faith is born in the announcing/personalization of the word. If faith is a fullness of adhering to the word, the soul necessarily must always fully relive the posture of listening. The divine-human mystery that forms the Christian is a synthesis of the word and its acceptance, of the seed that is scattered and the ground that receives it, of divine presentation and human reception.

The act of listening is a primary activity in every person, who by listening expresses a profound awareness of being a creature. Whoever receives everything from on high and sees all his own existential existence in the divine cannot help but adopt a posture of listening. Even before it serves as a means of communicating and receiving content, listening is the expression of life itself. It is an activity of one who delights in life and longs to communicate with others. The person who does not know how to listen or does not love to listen lives superficially. Personal existence unravels in the many tasks to accomplish, and the individual becomes a slave of haste and runs the risk of not having a firm foundation. But whoever listens reaches the golden rule of life: to lose oneself for the joy of the other and to rejoice in living quietly so that the other may develop fully in the great work of authentic, communal sharing.

The person who rejoices in being attentive to others will always find the courage to live, since that person is open to life and looks to the future. Such a person will not be wrapped up in the present anxiety but will look to a future rich with hope.

With such values the human being is ever more free of the distraction and deafness that impedes the word from communicating to the listener its truth. Listening is very important, since in every language that reaches the human heart there is created the condition for a rethinking, a critique, a conversion, an effective openness to the other. The one who listens loves communion and is predisposed to live it fully.

This state of soul represents the good soil for living the mystery of the covenant in which God turns to the people and the people proclaim their obedience. In such soil the scriptural tradition will produce much fruit.

Faith helps us hear anew the rich expressions from the Old Testament: "Hear, O Israel, the statutes and the ordinances that I am addressing to you today; you shall learn them and observe them diligently" (Deut 5:1). Faith leads us back to the spirituality of the pious Jew who every day repeated to himself and with his brothers: "Hear, O Israel: The LORD is our God, the LORD alone" (Deut 6:4). Faith carries us back to the habitual posture of the believer who blesses God incessantly in the proclamation of the good news. In the "Thanks be to God" that concludes the proclamation of the word in the liturgical assembly, the joy and the rich potential of listening are fully in us. Only in our attentive and loving listening does the word become life-giving, indicating the way to life.

Such a posture is a way of life for the believer, since that person has a thirst for the living God and longs for words that provide guidance. Were God never to respond, a void would be created in the heart of the community, making its listening nothing more than some interior drama. We know how in the Christian event God never ceases to address to us his message of salvation. Only when our hearts do not know how to accept the God who speaks inexhaustibly do we feel that God is mute. Our thirst for divine communication develops an interior attention in our daily life, creating the condition for our ritual listening.

Paying attention to the word thus became an expansion of our faith. The Lord loves the listening heart. Listening in the ordinary events of life, and in particular in the liturgical assembly, is the act of faith in the lordship of God who has liberated us from the slavery of sin and has introduced us to a living communion with the Infinite. Listening to God is a joy that invades the life of the believer.

Much of the liturgical celebration involves the faithful in listening, especially the proclamation of the Sacred Scriptures. In the ritual posture of listening we rediscover our vocation to be called, as the prophets were called, to feed on every word that flows from the mouth of God. The Christian who truly wishes to experience transfiguration in the Lord must be nourished by the word of God through understanding its meaning and must be in harmony with the Spirit, who causes us to be open to the Trinity's plan. If we wish to be people of the covenant in all our moments of existence, we must be disposed toward listening, to "eating" only the word that will fill our mouth with sweetness and will give us the strength for an untiring conversion. Though this word be bitter in the mouth, it soon will be transformed into blessedness by the gift of salvation.

The Christian knows that accepting the divine initiative in one's life means listening, following, being open to guidance. These are the characteristics of a person captured by the Lord's call.

True listening is entering into the existential dynamic both of a return to the sources of the speaker's choices and a desire to arrive at the speaker's goals. The listener follows in the footsteps of the Master, renounces autonomy, and testifies to the lordship of the one who calls. Such a conviction thus transforms this listening into continual supplication, asking that the Lord might reveal his demands to our hearts. The intensity of the gaze of the Master corresponds to the unconditional listening of the disciple.

Listening is not a simple auditory event but a placing of oneself before the gaze of the Master, which is operating in our existence and communicates to us the divine mystery so that we might live according to its teachings.

Thus listening becomes an authentic human and spiritual experience. To find the roots of our vocation in listening means to be receptive to the Creator through the Holy Spirit. We should be a living "Here I am" before God and sing of his life-giving fidelity in the word proclaimed in the liturgy and lived in daily life.

10

Striking One's Breast

The penitential posture is characteristic of the religious human being, and the gesture of striking one's breast calls attention to the penitent heart that longs in its humility for pardon. The liturgical celebration teaches the baptized to live one's vocation to conversion every day, since in that vocation one finds joy in God's mercy.

In the penitential rite of the Mass, there is this rubric: "The priest invites the people to recall their sins and to repent of them in silence. . . . All say: 'I confess to almighty God . . .' They strike their breast [as they say] 'that I have sinned through my own fault.'" We find such a sequence also in the rite of reconciliation at the moment of the confession of sins (cf. *Order of Penance* 54).

This gesture, which is found in every culture, has particular meaning for Christians. There are resonances that originate in the Gospels: "The time is fulfilled, and the kingdom of God has come near; repent, and believe in the good news" (Mark 1:15). "But when Simon Peter saw it, he fell down at Jesus' knees, saying: 'Go away from me, Lord, for I am a sinful man!'" (Luke 5:8). In the face of the great works of salvation, an attitude of repentance and conversion arises spontaneously. It is the attitude of the crowd at the foot of the cross: "And when all the crowds who had gathered there for this spectacle saw what had taken place, they returned home, beating their breasts" (Luke 23:48).

The Christian community, living in the context of celebrating the divine love present in the death and resurrection of Jesus, sees all the gravity of its own sin and presents to the Father its firm will for a radical conversion, cutting down at the roots whatever distances it from communion with the Father.

The origin of every sin is in the heart of the human being. That is Jesus' meaning when he affirms: "For it is from within, from the human heart, that evil intentions come" (Mark 7:21).

In the gesture of striking one's breast every baptized person, joined with the community in the sacramental celebration, confesses that the source of the noncommunion with God—the ground of one's life—is in the human heart: every existential lie with its own past, every non-acceptance of the paschal event through which one could become a new creation, every closeness to the Spirit who guides us in the ways of life and would animate our penitence. The psalm guides us here: "You desire truth in the inward being; / therefore teach me wisdom in my secret heart. . . . / Create in me a clean heart, O God, / and put a new and right spirit within me. . . . / The sacrifice acceptable to God is a broken spirit; / a broken and contrite heart, O God, you will not despise" (Ps 51:6, 10, 17). The divine light, rich in mercy, guides the penitential gesture.

Our hand here becomes the language for accusing the human heart, from which all evil that determines us arises. In this movement of the hand there is ideally a wringing of the heart of the "old self" in order to leave room for that of the new, as the prophet teaches: "A new heart I will give you, and a new spirit I will put within you; and I will remove from your body the heart of stone and give you a heart of flesh" (Ezek 36:26).

It is not enough to affirm a decisive will to convert the heart; a change of interior disposition is indispensable, as is an openness to being seized by God by leaving the source of any slavery. In this gesture of striking the breast all of the richness of paschal faith in the Lord is present, rooting itself in the heart of the disciple, converting that person to a new sensibility, and communicating all the possibilities of death and resurrection. There is nothing depressing at all about this gesture: there is no discounting of the person; there is no sadness about life. Rather, the song of hope implanted by the Spirit in the heart of the believer—who now lives in the revelation of God's love—retraces this act of faith in the mercy of God, underlining how already in the believer's consciousness of being distant from God that person is growing in communion with God. In that clenched hand that strikes the breast there is a willingness to shake off any spiritual laziness that might arise from the shadows of sin or from hardness of heart. There is a desire to knock down the wall of division that blocks the word from living in the heart of the Christian and educating that person according to the demands of the Spirit.

The person closed in heart and hardened through sin makes every decision bowing before the ego, a place dominated by the Evil One.

Striking thus his or her breast, this person desires to have a contrite and humble heart, the sacrifice that is pleasing to God. In this moment there arises from within the believer a prayer of supplication to the Spirit and in the Spirit, asking that the gifts of the sanctity and pardon of God might create that new heart that desires to live in the newness of life.

The gesture of striking one's breast thus is a deep act of faith that, operating by means of love, proclaims the creative goodness of God in the heart opened by penitence to the regenerating action of grace.

The condition of guilt that is present in the heart of the Christian on pilgrimage in this world is not an irreversible fact. There is always the possibility of divine newness that is generated by the faith that God presents to the person. The penitential gesture brings into focus a posture of confessing faith and of a profound sense of trust in the mercy of the Father. This gesture gives flesh to the person who, in firmly recognizing and increasingly affirming his or her own sinfulness ("through my own fault"), entrusts himself or herself fully to the goodness of God, proclaiming that mystery of death and resurrection that renews all things. It is the posture of faith of Peter, and it is the act of humility of the tax collector: "But the tax collector, standing far off, would not even look up to heaven, but was beating his breast and saying, 'God, be merciful to me, a sinner!'" (Luke 18:13).

And so Jesus' response to this posture of the tax collector sounds again in our own ears: "I tell you, this man went down to his home justified rather than the other; for all who exalt themselves will be humbled, but all who humble themselves will be exalted" (Luke 18:14).

The prayer of the community, concretized in the words of the priest, expresses the conviction that God is faithful to the penitent heart and continually enlivens it: "May almighty God have mercy on us, / forgive us our sins, / and bring us to everlasting life."

This humility of the community in understanding itself to be in a state of conversion in the Spirit is how God places a new heart in us. Every authentically religious person, in striking one's breast, asks that the mercy of God may renew and re-create us in God's true measure; for the sinner knows that there is justification by pure divine goodness.

11

Walking in Procession

The liturgical celebration involves processional gestures, for the procession of the people of God and the ministers parallels our continuous walk toward the eternal pastures of the kingdom. In this gesture we proclaim that we have here no fixed home, that we do not depend on any stability, since we know that life in all its meanings and relationships moves ever forward, that life is always in motion. Walking signifies life itself—searching, looking, deciding, departing toward that which gives meaning to existence. Such behavior is more than locomotion; it suggests the very meaning of life.

The person who walks is determined to reach the dreamed-for end of the way. To walk is to pray, to search, to thirst for an identity, to long for authentic human relationship. "Blessed are those who hunger and thirst for righteousness," Jesus would say (Matt 5:6). Our procession is authentic if it expresses that desire and carries it to action. Thus a procession cannot be distracted and routine, since that would reveal that superficiality reigns in our hearts, that we lack spiritual energy. In fact, the way we proceed along the various paths of life express our spiritual sensibility and energy. Our daily experiences are rich in this regard. Running can express joy and gaiety. Walking slowly can indicate concentration on thoughts that absorb the mind. Stopping can indicate the reaching of decisions. To walk again with enthusiasm can demonstrate that hope illuminates our mind and heart. Tired, dragging feet can indicate uncertainty as to how to construct the present, leading us to proceed moment by moment without great conviction. "Let me see how you walk and I will tell you the secret of your heart," might say the ancients. Proceeding in simplicity, gravity, and joy is proper to the person who is present before the Most High in the celebration, thus publicly affirming that his or her walk in life is in the Lord and is an ascension toward contemplating the Lord's face.

Our Christian identity is constructed on the conviction that we are pilgrims in this world. The walking of the believer underlines one's vocation to be a doer of the word (cf. Jas 1:22) in newness of life (cf. Rom 6:4), to live according to the Spirit (cf. Gal 5:25), to walk the paths of this world with the interior attitude of Abraham (cf. Heb 11:8ff.). The gift of being sons and daughters in the Son, taken up into the cloud of the Spirit, is not a gift to be held loosely, as if it were already fully acquired. The gift is rather to be developed slowly as a person assimilates the stature of Christ (cf. Eph 4:13). Every day the Truth draws us by conquering our heart and encourages us to seek the grace by which the Spirit enriches us moment by moment. The joy of being Christian is the joy of walking in the Truth (cf. 2 John), since we through the Father and in the Spirit are continually reclothed in Christ, placing us under Christ's living influence.

This human and Christian richness translates to celebrative language. We are not disembodied persons during the liturgy. Rather, our walking processionally is our way of proclaiming the faith that is in us and of professing consciously that we are under divine power, which alone makes it possible for us to live. Our walking is a prayer in action. We wish with all our strength to cry aloud, with the language of our body in movement, that we desire to grow in Christ in order to be fully in him, in conformity with the Pauline desire that Christ be all in all (cf. Col 3:11; Gal 3:27).

We live announcing the Gospel, an announcing that is a sharing of the mission of Jesus. He tells us every day: "Come to me, all you that are weary and are carrying heavy burdens, and I will give you rest" (Matt 11:28). Standing with him (cf. Mark 3:14) we make his command our own: "Go therefore and make disciples of all nations, baptizing them in the name of the Father and of the Son and of the Holy Spirit" (Matt 28:19).

Every day we are called to walk through the world's streets sharing Christ, who redeemed all humanity. The church must never remain still. It must go to all people and develop the charismatic and prophetic message of Pentecost, crying out to the world the presence of salvation.

Christ walks ahead of us and with us in order that we might with him bring salvation to our sisters and brothers, who themselves are searching for truth in their journey through time. As the church we are invited to relive the biblical exodus: to depart from the slavery of sin in order to proceed toward the Promised Land.

Such a journey animates all of our processional rites, because we live the passover of the Lord, the passage from death to life. We proceed in obedience to God since, as disciples of the Lord, we are called in every instant to live God's wisdom and to develop the gift of communion with the Father. Our journey in time as followers of Christ is toward this goal. When our earthly pilgrimage is finished and when we begin to follow the Lamb (cf. Rev 14:1ff.) in the heavenly Jerusalem, we will sing the new song that will be our eternal realization. Our ritual procession as well as the journey of our life will continue in eternity. Our souls, at the end of their journey in following the Master, will be clothed anew with the fullness of light.

To learn to walk is to learn to grow in the sense of life and to give flesh to the joy of living that will enable us to walk eternally in the presence of the Holy Trinity. In the liturgy we pass continually from time to eternity, wrapped up in the paschal mystery and pressed by the Spirit. This is our processional walking in the liturgical assembly.

12

Observing

The human eye has an important role in communication. It is a mirror of the inner person and of one's relationship with created beauty. Such sensitive richness occurs also in the life of the church in order to give living flesh to faith in the Christian community. In its expressive language the liturgy calls for visual attention by the assembly, who participates actively also by watching and observing.

Ritual has a dimension of observation, which is an instrument of perceiving an event mediated by sign. However, we must not merely watch the rite, forgetting all of the vitality present in the sacramental event that calls for a contemplation of the Lord present among his own. In fact, to only watch could cause one to lose the spiritual and symbolic message that animates and defines liturgical language. We are called to rejoice in the celebrative sign, a marvelous synthesis of the Invisible and the visible, in order to contemplate the event. The evangelist John continually reminds his hearers not to remain at a mere external level but to enter into the mystery. That is made possible by the action of the same life-giving Spirit who works in the hearts of believers, since "It is the spirit that gives life; the flesh is useless" (John 6:63).

Ritual action has as its specific function to bring the brothers and sisters gathered in faith to consciousness that God is close to the people and that they are close to God, thus developing that eschatological anxiousness that leads the community to long to enjoy fully the face of the Father. In our sacramental walk we gather to see in faith, as the apostle Paul teaches us: "So we are always confident; even though we know that while we are at home in the body we are away from the Lord—for we walk by faith, not by sight" (2 Cor 5:6-7).

The Lord is sacramentally present in our midst, though physically absent. Our vision is stimulated immediately by the ritual, but it is more deeply stimulated by the richness of faith to enter into the whole salvific and paschal significance of the rite in order to contemplate the mystery. This ineffable experience is possible because the baptized person forms his or her own vision along the deep, daily current of faith.

We know how a gaze that expresses the interiority of a person enters into communion with that of others, creating an increase in the communion that exists between them. That process also happens in our relationship with the divine. Through the whole celebration this process, supported by the Spirit, is attentive to what God is revealing and leads the celebrants to rejoice in an intense communion with the Divine Persons. Such an intent is rooted in the gift of the gaze of Christ to the disciples. Turning to the disciples at the moment of their call, Jesus totally won them to his mission: "As Jesus passed along the Sea of Galilee, he saw Simon and his brother casting a net into the sea. . . . And Jesus said to them, 'Follow me. . . .' And immediately they left their nets and followed him" (Mark 1:16-18). Whoever lives from and in the gaze of the Lord sees and follows.

Love is communicated through the eyes. The assembly, being called together in the power and in the light of the Spirit, is thus able to grasp the profound reality of the event. In fact, the eye brings the distant close and discovers a vast part of the world for us. Since the eye also searches for the Absolute, the communion of the Absolute places the person in the life of God, to live in a constant condition of purification, transfiguration, and glorification. Such is the richness that we taste when in the assembly we participate in the gift of salvation and take active part in the celebration. The celebration reveals the truth of the Gospel message: "But blessed are your eyes, for they see, and your ears, for they hear. Truly I tell you, many prophets and righteous people longed to see what you see, but did not see it, and to hear what you hear, but did not hear it" (Matt 13:16-17).

In fact, just as the eye is attracted to light, so is the creature attracted to the Creator. The soul that longs for the Infinite is filled by the Infinite that sacramentally manifests itself. Its gaze is satisfied by the manifestation of divine goodness. The anxiousness for the Eternal involves the person in celebration. Through the eye we see the Light, we accept it, and we allow it to penetrate our souls. In the Light we are light, and as light we grasp the presence of the divine luminosity.

The ritual posture of observing is not passivity; rather, it is the expression of a person's heart. "The eye is the lamp of the body. So, if your eye is healthy, your whole body will be full of light; but if your eye is unhealthy, your whole body will be full of darkness. If then the light in you is darkness, how great is the darkness!" (Matt 6:22-23).

To observe actively and consciously the habitual unfolding of the sacramental event is an exercise of purity of heart that carries the baptized to "see God." This interior condition helps us realize that while we see the rite we glimpse also the Lord, since a consciousness of the presence of God rooted in faith penetrates our spirit. In the celebration we see that for which we search, the heart senses that which it loves, it contemplates that which the spirit desires.

Our entrance into the celebrating assembly is animated by a theological orientation toward Christ Jesus: "let us run with perseverance the race that is set before us, looking to Jesus the pioneer and perfecter of our faith" (Heb 12:1-2).

Our watching during the liturgical celebration, while it fascinates our senses, helps us taste how sweet and gentle, rich in fidelity and in mercy, is the Lord. The light of the rite, while it catches the eyes of the flesh inebriates those of the Spirit and leads us to adore the immense greatness of the paschal love of the Lord.

The eye is also for supplication. In the celebration we pray with our eyes: "Come, Lord Jesus!" It is that which Psalm 121 teaches us, where the invitation to look into the heights makes us understand that salvation comes only from the Most High: "I lift up my eyes to the hills— / from where will my help come? / My help comes from the LORD, / who made heaven and earth" (Ps 121:1-2).

The eyes express clearly the desire of the heart, its anxieties, its expectations, and consequently, its joys and its sorrows. In the celebration we have our gaze fixed on the Most High, since God alone is our rock of salvation and our hope.

With this at our core, our gaze will never be dominated by temptations that orient us toward that which is only visible, will not suffer distractions that turn us toward that which is marginal. For the gaze of the believer does not remain fixed on the things that pass. Rather, the seeing that takes place in the liturgy emerges in the Infinite and tastes the salvation that comes from the Lord.

The ritual action thus carries us to live John 19:35: "He who saw this has testified so that you also may believe. His testimony is true, and he knows that he tells the truth." Thus the joy of the observer will translate itself into the joy of "sacramentally seeing" the Lord in expectation of full vision in the glory of the saints.

13

Singing

Singing belongs to all people, and the church has made this language its own. The Constitution on the Sacred Liturgy underlines the truth that sacred music is a necessary part of the solemn liturgy (cf. *Sacrosanctum Concilium* 112), since it fosters the full and active participation of the whole assembly of the faithful (cf. *Sacrosanctum Concilium* 30).

The joy of singing is not a merely external fact; it is the rich manifestation of the spirit of every human being. That which is in our heart is expressed in the joy, the freshness, or the suffering of language. To sing expresses the exaltation of the spirit before the beautiful, testifying to the lyricism of the heart enthralled by the Ineffable. In fact, when the human spirit is taken up emotionally by beauty, it can only turn to song to express itself. The human spirit—fascinated with its surroundings—is filled with joy, experiences an interior liberty, and can only cry out with joy in its own spiritual vitality. That which has taken form in the person's spirit and soul is manifested in song.

Such happens not only when we are happy but also when we are sad. Singing underlines the inexhaustible hope of the human heart and allows it to look with serenity on life's difficulties, even the gravest ones, that from time to time suffocate its strong desire to live. The human being who does not want to sing can be tempted to become enclosed in individualism and does not succeed in grasping the beauty of life gained through the intensity of interpersonal relationships.

Singing is the voice of joy and hope. It expresses a living and rich rapport with the Absolute, and it gives flesh to that experience, which transcends the human being. Through singing we express various states of soul, whether they are joyful or tormented, in order to grow in that interior harmony that helps us communicate with our world.

When we sing, the whole of our person finds its interior unity and breathes an intense breath of life in the enthusiasm of creating a new world. Melodious expression lives from a rich context of transcendence. It roots itself in communion with the Absolute, and it gives voice to a living and strong dialogue with the Ineffable. It is that which the psalms propose to us over and over again: "Sing to the Lord a new song," particularly in the celebration of Morning Prayer. In the appearance of the light that conquers the shadows, the soul takes notice of the divine fidelity that once again calls humanity into existence, into the light, into relationships, and into a rich experience of communion. That new song emerges from a heart that understands how great is the goodness of the Lord who every day calls all things into existence, making them pass from the obscurity of night into the brightness of day. The voice of the human being who gives shape to the interior song is a living manifestation of purity of heart, a crying out of the uncontestable divine fullness that lives in every person. Singing tells us how the fullness of the heart overflows.

Song, however, is not an end in itself but pursues the intent of every person to communicate with the divine. Singing in its linguistic-anthropological dynamic helps us to come out of ourselves, to forget ourselves. It is the beauty of the song that attracts us. To sing is to enter the ecstasy of beauty. "Sing and walk," Augustine says to his community, underlining how the presence of the Eternal is a source of energy that helps a person overcome obstacles and enter into the fullness of life. The very sound of a voice turned toward the heights indicates how the Ineffable can conquer the heart of a human being, causing inspiration, so that the language that emerges may unite the world of the heart with the divine. In this sense one can say that singing is a twofold prayer, since it underlines the divine communion that is true prayer. The one who sings is master of time because he or she breathes eternity.

Such openness to God educates a person. Singing, along with reflection, allows for the slow penetration of truth in one's spirit, making the singer realize a living relationship with God that can root itself firmly in his spirit.

The person who sings abdicates any defense of the ego and is shaped by the messages being sung, allowing himself or herself to become a luminous image of God. Spoken language cannot always succeed in expressing this experience. This liberty that progressively constructs itself reemerges as jubilant singing, as Augustine tells us:

"To understand and to not know how to explain in words that which is sung with the heart. . . . Jubilation is that melody, with which the heart speaks what it does not succeed to express in words. . . . The heart will open itself to joy, without being served by words, and the extraordinary greatness of this joy will not know the limitations of syllables." To sing is a sign of the ineffable fullness that overflows from a heart that is truly joyful.

To sing is to express the communion and the choral truth that animates the Christian community in its depth, according to the beautiful invitation of the apostle Paul: "Let the word of Christ dwell in you richly; teach and admonish one another in all wisdom, and with gratitude in your hearts sing psalms, hymns, and spiritual songs to God" (Col 3:16).

When singing gives visibility to the faith that unites the saints, it expresses the communion of the church. In the assembly we rejoice in a believed, sung, and witnessed faith for the benefit of all humanity, and in this way we live the union for which Christ gave his life and by which he continues to be present in the midst of his people. Thus singing, correctly understood, is not a simple exterior gesture that sometimes expresses also human vanity; rather, it gives credence to all the tonalities of the spirit, incarnating our innate sense of beauty. Singing is the strength of hope that operates in the interior of the person; it is openness to the transcendent, on which the person is modeled in view of the fullness of that melodious experience sketched in the book of Revelation: "And I heard a voice from heaven like the sound of many waters and like the sound of loud thunder; the voice I heard was like the sound of harpists playing on their harps, and they sing a new song before the throne and before the four living creatures and before the elders. No one could learn that song except the one hundred and forty-four thousand who have been redeemed from the earth" (14:2-3). In the heavenly Jerusalem singing will be the great celebration of the fullness of life.

14

Baptismal Bathing

Water fascinates the mind and heart, since one's image and its surroundings may be reflected in it. The colors and movements, the qualities present in water, call forth various thoughts and sentiments. Water can reflect the beautiful images that enthrall the imagination of persons and stimulate poets.

It is significant that in religious forms all over the world water has always had a particularly remarkable place. It is a sign of the pureness of life that is a profound aspiration of people. The place where water is gathered becomes the sign of how such a gift is concretely offered. In it one can be immersed, finding new life, freshness, restoration. Such richness translates into a figurative language that acquires immediate symbolic value.

Water is the font of life. How could we live without water? As everything that lives is born from water, so also by means of water that very gift of life is conserved. This is what the sacred author teaches when he tells us of the creation of the world (cf. Gen 1:1, 4-10, 20-22). If there were no rain what would become of nature? If a person could not drink, how could the body be supported? The joy of seeing water and, above all, seeing the running water of mountain streams and waterfalls becomes a hymn to life. Everything recovers fertility and strength from water. In water death dies and life reflowers.

The church, observing the nature of water, rediscovers the meaning of the baptismal sign of immersion/emersion, of entering into death in order to exit rich with life. In this immersion/emersion all the qualities of water become evident. The church, wanting to signify the new life that Christ offers to all humanity, has placed this richness in the baptismal bathing. The baptismal font is a fountain of life, from which emerges the new creature and where the "old self" with its negative baggage dies to sin, to become the new creature created in God's image, as the apostle Paul teaches us: "you have stripped off the old self with its practices and have clothed yourselves with the new self, which is being renewed in knowledge according to the image of its creator" (Col 3:9-10), since "you were washed, you were sanctified, you were justified in the name of the Lord Jesus Christ and in the Spirit of our God" (1 Cor 6:11).

This event takes places because the richness of the water is the fruit of the Spirit, which "penetrates" the waters of the baptismal font and allows the person to be reborn from on high, by water and the Holy Spirit. That work of regeneration is a bath renewing the whole person. In contact with Christ, we share his death and resurrection, abandoning the old person and reclothing ourselves as the new.

In the baptismal font God creates an adorer of the Father in spirit and truth. Water creates and re-creates the one who is there immersed, and the pure human being reemerges purified, sanctified, justified, glorified. In that water the whole process of the history of salvation is realized. The prayer of blessing the baptismal water reminds us of creation, destruction, redemption. Thus the baptismal water brings us to relive the beginnings of the history of humanity.

By means of water, from the chaos of the cosmos there emerged nature with all its abundance, the flowering of plant life, the vitality of the animals and of the sky, the earth and the waters of the sea, and the exultance of the being created in the image and likeness of God. And of all this, in the evening, God said, "It is all good!"

The baptismal bath invites us to understand this regeneration as the beginning of that new world that is the heart of the baptized. Water also assumes the meaning of destruction in the example of the flood, since its force has the capacity to batter everything it encounters. How many times have excessive rains caused all forms of life to be lost! The baptized is called to abandon definitively the "old self" who is opposed to true life by means of the sign of immersion in water, so that a new humanity can flourish in love and in peace. The baptismal gift impels us to bury sin in order that the gift of grace may flower.

In a word, water indicates the passage, the passover, the passing through the Red Sea. Slavery is at last abandoned and annulled, and the faithful one advances to the mystery of freedom. The baptismal font is where the true exodus from slavery is celebrated, and it reminds us how the journey of the disciple of the Lord should be a continuous conversion: a passage from the shadows into the light. Our existence becomes biblical. The water in the sacred font represents the incarnation of the mighty works of God who wants to lead every human being to salvation. In those waters we discover the truest meaning of walking in the ways of life. In the font we are immersed in the communication of the divine life. By means of water we die to the old Adam, and we discover the new Adam.

That gesture of immersion/emersion in the baptismal font is the song of the joy of God and of humanity, of those who see a new world being born, a new gift of the Spirit for the freshness of the community. It is an act of divine fidelity that calls all human beings to be the Father's daughters and sons in the Son and to sing the beauties of nature living in harmony with the creative will.

The baptismal font represents for us the maternal sense of the church that generates new sons and daughters for the glory of the Father and for the construction of a humanity in which communion, freedom, and praise can shine.

15

Sprinkling

On the Lord's Day the beginning of the eucharistic celebration is sometimes marked by the blessing of the water with which the assembly will be sprinkled and which may then be placed in the holy water fonts near the doors of the church. The rite of sprinkling represents a remembering of the event that has determined the life of every member of the community in the celebration of baptism.

Immersion in water has effected our birth. Every year in the Easter Vigil our baptism is remembered; every Sunday, a weekly Easter, we relive that mystery. The introduction to the ritual of the blessing of holy water affirms: "On the basis of age-old custom, water is one of the signs that the Church often uses in blessing the faithful. Holy water reminds the faithful of Christ, who is given to us as the supreme divine blessing, who called himself the living water, and who in water established baptism for our sake as the sacramental sign of the blessing that brings salvation" (*Book of Blessings* 1388).

"The blessing and sprinkling of holy water usually take place on Sunday, in keeping with the rite given in the Roman Missal" (*Book of Blessings* 1389). The newness and richness that baptism has produced in the heart of every person runs the risk of not being sufficiently deepened and personalized in daily life.

Born in God we become every day sons and daughters of God in order to reach the maturity of faith. The Sunday ritual of sprinkling reminds us of that ineffable mystery and presents us, always in a new way, with the demands of the paschal gift for a new life, so that in Christ we will know every day to die and rise. A lifestyle that should be continually attentive to invisible realities—such is the mystery of the resurrection of the Lord—needs signs that recall the mystery that has defined our lives and call us to consistency of life. This richness becomes very clear in the gesture of sprinkling with blessed water. By this gesture we are immersed again in that river of living water that flows from the right side of the temple and makes all things new: "Wherever the river goes, every living creature that swarms will live. . . . It will become fresh; and everything will live where the river goes. . . . On the banks, on both sides of the river, there will grow all kinds of trees for food. Their leaves will not wither nor their fruit fail, but they will bear fresh fruit every month, because the water for them flows from the sanctuary. Their fruit will be for food, and their leaves for healing" (Ezek 47:9, 12).

This prophecy is fully realized in Jesus who died on the cross, when from his side blood and water flowed (cf. John 19:34) and the disciples were filled by his Spirit (cf. John 7:37-39). The antiphonal texts for the Easter season enlighten us and give us confirmation: "Behold the water, that flows from the holy temple of God, alleluia; and to many it will come and this water will bring salvation, and they will sing: alleluia, alleluia." "From your side, Christ our Lord, a fountain of salvation had flowed and it washes us from sin, and renews life in all the world. Alleluia."

A recalling of Ezekiel 36:25-26 animates the antiphon for outside the Easter season, indicating the spiritual newness that baptism produces: "Over you will flow pure water, and you will be cleansed from every sin, and I will give you a new heart, says the Lord."

The procession of the priest into the nave of the church, in fact, brings to life the spreading forth of this spiritual water that changes the heart of human beings, brings the joy of the messianic times, and renews faith in the benevolence of the Father. We sense ourselves immersed again in the baptismal font, and our whole person feels fully consecrated to God.

Such a gesture, at the beginning of the celebration, reminds us that on the day of our baptism we became one with Christ, dead and risen. Now we are his memorial, since Christ is contemporary to us and we to him. Today's ritual is an expression of our mystical and sacramental dying and rising in the Lord. In this moment we celebrate his passover by sacrament because he makes us participants in the mystery of his death and resurrection by means of the sacred rite. At times we may be tempted to live this calling together of the liturgical assembly either passively, or to think that we are its protagonists. The sprinkling, however, reminds us that we are exercising our priestly service, just as the baptismal rite teaches, when at the moment of anointing it recalls that we join Christ, priest, king, and prophet. Christ in us, with us, and for us actualizes that paschal event that defines our existence.

That the sprinkling may take the place of the penitential rite reminds us that the celebration is for those who rejoice in the remission of sins offered in the death of the Lord to the one who lives the newness of Easter. Inundated by the water of salvation, we approach the altar of the Lord with greater consciousness, to be a part of his paschal oblation. In the house of a sick person the celebration of the sacraments may be preceded by a sprinkling, accompanied by these words: "Let this water call to mind our baptism into Christ, / who by his death and resurrection has redeemed us." That baptismal water has the strength, the capacity, and the fitness to place the sign of Christ in a way that is true and rich.

Such a rite becomes a frequent experience with the blessing with holy water we make with faith and simplicity whenever we enter church. At all the entrances holy water fonts contain blessed water. Dipping our hand in the water, we symbolically enter again the baptismal waters, and in the sign of the cross we remind ourselves that it is only by means of baptism that we are sons and daughters of God, whose family is the church. It is baptism that introduces us into the Christian community and offers us true dignity with its accompanying moral demand: "You shall be holy, for I, the LORD your God, am holy" (cf. 1 Pet 1:15-16; Lev 11:44). Making the sign of the cross with holy water reminds us who we effectively are and what daily efforts we must make to live such richness.

Last, sprinkling accompanies the blessing of persons and things. Such a ritual reminds us that we should always walk in the spirit of the passover of the Lord and that only in Easter do we have a point of reference for our daily choices. Blessing with water objects that we use in our daily lives reminds us that they must be used for the good, in such a way that our ordinary lives—in all their complexity—may conform to the will of the Father.

Welcoming the sprinkling of holy water, we place ourselves within that river of living water that is the paschal love of the Lord in order to be ever more new creatures who renew our brothers and sisters and the cosmos so that the glory of the Father may rise in all creation.

16

Laying on of Hands

Placing a hand on the head of a person, especially a baby, is a common gesture. It attempts to express the feeling of not wanting a person to be alone. To lay hands on the head of a baby is to communicate tenderness, to inspire trust, to make the baby feel like a person, to engage life. Such a gesture is repeated throughout life, since every person senses the need for a living, genuine, and fruitful relationship with a brother or sister in order to grow in trust and hope. People have a strong need for communion with others.

The laying on of hands demands that the one who makes the gesture also be a fitting source of the trust that is communicated. In fact, it is the more mature person who lays on hands. It is God who lets power, by the sign of the laying on of hands by the minister, descend upon the heads of the people so that everyone may rejoice in the truth of divine life. In this moment there is a communion between heaven and earth.

The hand in its vitality expresses a person's heat and energy, his or her state of soul and expectations. The hand is never only a little expressive. It expresses the heart of the human being as it says to another, "You are not alone; I am with you."

Such a gesture comes to the liturgy from Scripture. The sacraments come from God and regenerate the person. In ritual the Father communicates the salvation of Easter to the community so that the faithful may walk in new life. Alone we cannot truly and fully reach the Absolute or fulfill the mission that Christ has entrusted to us of spreading the Gospel across the world.

Imposing hands on the head of a person underlines the action of divine benevolence that descends upon a person and makes that person a sign of the passover of Jesus. The sign communicates divine life and establishes the communion between God and the one who receives it. It is the "today" of Pentecost. Every time we lay hands on a person or receive the imposition of hands, we rejoice in the certainty that God is again with us.

A simple gesture often communicates more than do words, but words always accompany gestures, such as the laying on of hands in the sacraments of ordination and the anointing of the sick. During these sacraments the laying on of hands is done while the minister prays that God may bless the person receiving the sacrament.

The laying on of hands is an authentic spiritual experience in the life of the church. In that gesture we contemplate the God of messianic gifts and the person who is present before God with empty hands, hoping for salvation. The person raises his palms upward, while the celebrant, representing God, has his palms turned downward: the one is waiting, enriched through prayer; the other in generosity fills the recipient with divine gifts.

It is always beautiful to recall Jesus' regard for children: "Then little children were being brought to him in order that he might lay his hands on them and pray. . . . Jesus said, 'Let the little children come to me, and do not stop them; for it is to such as these that the kingdom of heaven belongs.' And he laid his hands on them and went on his way" (Matt 19:13-15). Jesus gives his spirit to the one who is small, so that—clothed in Jesus' light—that person may become the greatest in the kingdom.

In making this same gesture with simplicity and humility, the Christian brings alive again the feelings of the Master in everyday life. In the sacraments this laying on of hands acquires a particular salvific importance. The imposition of hands is the creating gesture of the Spirit, renewing whoever celebrates the event of Easter in the sign of penitence with a contrite heart. In confirmation the fullness of divine communion reaches the faithful so that they might proclaim to the world the mighty works of divine love. The effusion of divine hope in the silent laying on of hands during the anointing of the sick strengthens the heart of the sick person as it struggles with the sufferings of the present. The laying on of hands becomes a simple and rich gesture of communion by the person who places his or her hands on the sick person, indicating a sharing in that person's burdens and letting that person know that he or she is not alone in carrying such burdens.

The duty that we Christians take up on leaving the liturgical assembly may be accompanied by a laying on of hands, so that the wealth of the Spirit may nourish our daily existence, giving us the strength to follow the Gospel and to be charitable and kind in the ordinary relationships of life. The gesture of laying on of hands tells us that God is always present and will not disappoint us. The sacramental language of laying on of hands thus points to the divine assistance for the Christian community and to the conviction that the Spirit is always living and life-giving, helping the believer grow in freedom, obedience, and divine communion.

17

Anointing

The gesture of anointing is fairly common among various cultures, whether from a therapeutic point of view or as an indication of a person's emotional state, for example, joy and richness. Anointing also has a wide range of practices and meanings in the celebration of the sacraments.

In the tradition of the Old Testament the gesture of anointing indicated a sense of election by God and thus a consciousness of belonging to God. The act of anointing emphasized that the person was chosen as one particularly blessed by God, so that that person might proceed in the mission God had assigned, such as the missions of kings and prophets. The Most High chose people as envoys to pursue certain tasks, and through anointing a person received the energy to pursue these tasks.

The gesture of anointing possesses a particular symbolic meaning. The oil passes from the skin into the body. The heat thus generated places the muscles in optimal condition to follow the commands of the will. The oil warms the muscles, making them malleable and agile, as in the experience of athletes.

Such an example is helpful for the person who is called to do the will of God. The history of salvation, with respect to this sign, gives particular significance to the gesture of anointing: the person is put in the position of docility before God. In fact, sacramental actions represent the communication of the mystery of the Father and the mission of Christ in his church: the faithful are united in Christ so that they may operate and cooperate in the salvation of the people of God.

The life of Jesus had numerous references to anointing. Jesus is defined in Scripture as the "anointed one" of the Father. He is the one on whom the Father has placed his favor, so that he may realize that hour in which all humanity will be redeemed and will be formed into one single people to the praise and glory of the Father. In Jesus new times have appeared: from him the word goes forth that regenerates the hearts of people. Around him the messianic community is created in joy and exaltation. Christ was "anointed" by the Father, so that he would be perfectly open to the Father's wishes, carrying to its fulfillment the mission he received: it is that which Jesus did in the mystery of the cross, in which everything is completed (see John 19:30). He was anointed by the Holy Spirit, so that the Paraclete, from the very morning of existence, could be attentive to the wishes of the Father and could communicate to human beings the divine faithfulness. Anointing thus represents a continual sacramental recalling to openness toward God and trust in God's operative power.

The communication of the Holy Spirit is also signified in this gesture of anointing (cf. 1 John 2:20, 27). It is the Spirit who knows the wishes of the Father (cf. 1 Cor 2:10), communicates them, and offers the capacity to make them concrete in everyday life. The Spirit penetrates the hearts of disciples and make them new, so that they may be rich in divine love through openness to the Spirit's action. In the gesture of anointing we contemplate the fulfillment of a great mystery: the Spirit enters the disciple and unfolds there all the Spirit's possibilities so that the soul may give full assent to the divine thought and not become discouraged in the daily difficulties of life. To anoint is to help a person stand in the hand of God and to be obedient to the wishes of Christ and his Father.

To live in this way is difficult because of our imprisonment by sin. The Spirit, by means of the spreading of the oil on our heads or elsewhere on our bodies, strengthens and comforts us, leading us toward that heroic freedom that is a gift from on high, giving us the courage of the Pentecost community and of the church of the martyrs. This is important because our earthly reality is bristling with dangers, obstacles, and conflicts with the Evil One. The prebaptismal anointing thus signifies the gift of the Spirit that makes the Christian ready for battle and offers certainty that the divine favor will not lessen. While we must face the temptations of the devil, anointing gives us the certainty that the Spirit will help us fight temptation, and if we are open to that Spirit, we will be victorious.

The anointing of the sick reveals the divine action that strengthens us and helps us understand the will of the Father. The Spirit helps the sick person to live the tragic moment of grave infirmity as a part of God's purpose. From this there can come either physical healing or the courage to pass serenely into eternal happiness. Anointing proclaims above all an interior healing in the face of the tremendous difficulties that arise in the heart of the sick person. The ritual of anointing reminds the sick of the power of the resurrection.

Finally, anointing is a sign of joy, of richness and exuberance, since it underlines the fullness of the gifts of the soul that make it capable to witness the Gospel with one's life, even as far as martyrdom, in freedom and with courage. It is the very dynamic of the sacrament of confirmation in which the Spirit completes the work that the Father began in baptism, so that the faithful may proclaim the advent of messianic times even in ordinary life.

In anointing, the seven gifts of the Spirit that make the heart of the baptized particularly attentive to God are present. The Spirit expresses readiness, obedience, security, proclamation, and freedom. It is the Spirit who speaks in everyone who has been reborn. The gesture of anointing offers divine warmth to the human person, tired from sin, so that the presence of God may be welcomed and we might give witness to the kingdom before the world.

18

Praying

Through prayer we live each day as creatures made in the image and likeness of God, and through prayer we express our welcome of salvation in Jesus Christ. The sacramental encounter between God and the assembly lives from the power of prayer that sustains every ritual moment, since this spiritual wealth underlines, on the one hand, the rich poverty of the suppliant assembly and, on the other, the salvific freedom of God the Father, Son, and Holy Spirit that is provided the faithful. Prayer expresses the living awareness of the faithful of being in the presence of God and enwrapped in the cloud of God's power.

The assembly lives through acknowledging its own poverty, as the psalm affirms: "The eyes of the LORD are on the righteous, / and his ears are open to their cry. / . . . When the righteous cry for help, the LORD hears, / and rescues them from all their troubles" (Ps 34:15, 17).

The faithful find joy in presenting themselves to God with empty hands because the Most High is the substance of their whole life, the fullness of their being. Through praying we place ourselves before God and present the concerns of our daily life. We express fidelity to the power of God and our delight in the events of Easter and Pentecost, to the mission of Christ and the apostles, to the longing for salvation through the guidance of the Spirit, and to the certainty of redemption.

To pray is to make present the intention of the psalmist who lives only in rapport with God: "O God, you are my God, I seek you, / my soul thirsts for you; / my flesh faints for you, / as in a dry and weary land where there is no water" (Ps 63:1).

This vitality shows itself in the gestures of ritual, which even in their multiplicity and complexity are thoroughly imbued with prayer in sacramental celebration. The bodily languages of prayer bring to light the feelings that animate the assembly gathered in prayer, languages brought together in one single spirit: that of the poor one standing before the Most High.

In standing we demonstrate that prayer is an act of faith and a prophetic sign of the great event of the resurrection that gives life to the community. In kneeling we let spring forth the adoration of the Ineffable and we recognize our penitence that leads us to rejoice in conversion. In sitting we send forth our expectation that our souls before God might be filled with Christ. In joined hands we concentrate on the mystery of God who longs to penetrate our hearts. In arms raised in thanks and praise our prayer recognizes the lordship of God over each of us in our community. In our processional walks we give witness to the pilgrimage of the church that lives in the certainty of God's providence. In singing and playing musical instruments, we celebrate the wonders of God.

This multiplicity of gestures gives witness to the assembly's wanting to live with God. The assembly is a gathering of the faithful, regenerated from the waters of the Holy Spirit and a living sign of the face of Christ. Praying helps the gathered faithful be conscious of their vocation and expresses their daily acceptance of God's will. Praying makes the assembly open to God so that it may be molded by the Spirit in rich imitation of Christ for the praise and glory of the Father.

Through the church the faithful learns to pray in an authentic way. While our culture all too often loves verbosity, needless images, complexity, noise and clamor, which surround us with vanity instead of introducing us to the Absolute, authentic liturgical prayer, in contemplating God and the wonders of God, chooses instead what is most essential. It proclaims that the one and triune God is the Lord of life and of our human history. It develops inner prayer, since in celebrating the liturgy we express the heart and mind of God. Liturgy celebrates the humble and contrite heart that is a sacrifice pleasing to God. Such authentic prayer longs for simplicity because it communicates the presence of God in our lives. The liturgy is our daily school of prayer.

Being in assembly educates the Christian to be oriented toward God. An assembly that loves what is essential and what is simple, that rejoices in contemplation and values meditation, through the Spirit recognizes the liturgy as communal prayer. It is difficult to pray in an assembly when such values are not present in the hearts of the faithful, who do not let themselves be molded by the liturgy.

Moreover, liturgical praying loves to underline the "we." We are the people of God on pilgrimage who in the one faith accept, ask, sing, and testify. Despite our individual differences, within the liturgical assembly we express a unity that is animated by the Redeemer, who communicates the paschal life to all of us.

While our egos keep us from always being in harmony with Christ and with the Spirit who makes us participants in God's freedom, our prayer in the assembly gives us the joy of forgetting ourselves, of giving space within our hearts and minds to the Master, of being able to find ourselves with all our brothers and sisters in offering to the Father one single prayer, an expression of a people who rediscovers itself in the unity of God, Father, Son, and Holy Spirit.

To pray in the liturgy becomes an exercise of our baptismal priesthood that expands, develops, and communicates, and thus creates the process of maturation in faith that is the goal of our communal prayer.

19

Blessing

One of the signs that frequently accompanies the concluding rites of sacramental celebrations is the gesture of blessing: "And may the blessing of almighty God, / the Father, and the Son, and the Holy Spirit, / come upon you and remain with you for ever." In expressing the trinitarian text the minister traces the sign of the cross over the gathered faithful, who accept it by making the sign of the cross on their persons. Its meaning becomes even clearer at the end of a prayer, as is the case in the celebration of the sacraments or the sacramentals. Prayer is the true expression of blessing, since in it the desire of the community is expressed, and in it the community is filled with God's power. The sign of the cross makes evident how the benevolence of the Father shows itself by means of the cross. The Christian who lives by the cross lives from the divine abundance and becomes a place for God's blessings. The religious gesture of blessing has its place in every religious expression of whatever time and place.

In ancient cultures the father of a family would bless his children. Such a gesture signified the continuity of the life and spirit of the family. As humans we desire to be blessed; the word itself conveys health, prosperity, and joy in life. Underlying a blessing is the conviction that life is a gift, that it comes from on high and represents divine life in the reality of every day.

Regrettably, some fear not receiving God's blessings. Such fears may be put aside in the knowledge that the blessing of God will be provided all who ask for it. God will not abandon us. God will assist us, will answer our prayers, and will share eternal life with us. God's blessing distances us from evil, since the power that comes from on high breaks down the powers of evil.

The liturgy is a great blessing that points to the primacy of God: God is the source of everything that exists, of the whole process of salvation and of its fulfillment. Through ritual we celebrate that loving face of God turned toward humanity. By means of blessing we are called to share this divine power so that we may proclaim to the whole world the unfathomable marvels of God.

Faith helps us to understand that we are blessed and that our existence belongs to the Creator. Paul's hymn of the ancient church teaches us: "Blessed be the God and Father of our Lord Jesus Christ, who has blessed us in Christ with every spiritual blessing in the heavenly places, just as he chose us in Christ" (Eph 1:3). We bless the Lord, so that the Lord's benevolence may always be actual in our life. Such a conviction emerges in the very attitude with which we receive the divine blessing.

When we receive a blessing, we bow down or we kneel. By means of this gesture we profess our faith: everything comes from the Father in Christ and in the Spirit, since we all come from God in order to live according to the wishes of God. If God were not to bless us, we could not follow all of God's desires. We could not make God's concrete will actual, and especially in our daily life we would not be able to live in the wisdom of the cross, which is the single interpretative key of our existence.

Only the one who is in God lives this divine wisdom. This we grasp above all at the end of every sacramental celebration in which we have participated in the death and resurrection of the Lord. God the Father in the liturgical sign fills us again with benevolence and fills our soul with his Spirit so that we will know how to live our lives according to the Gospel.

Blessed by grace and aware of this gift, we live our lives glorifying and imitating the Lord, certain that God will enrich us. Blessing brings us the grace of life and teaches us to follow the divine will in our every moment. This same life-with-God that is life itself for the Christian is a blessing in action. We live as blessed ones when faith-hope-love is the heart of every moment the Father offers us.

The person who lives these convictions knows how to walk in a newness of life where God's presence never disappoints. Such richness of life, however, reminds us of our limitations. If blessing is a grace, then our richness grows from a heart that is poor but rich with prayer, knowing that we could not exist even for one moment if it were not for God's grace. It is this grace that enables us to grow in faith and to reflect the life of the risen Christ.

The act of blessing is not magic. It does not reduce itself to a simple mechanical gesture but lives in the heart of a person who turns his or her face toward God, who desires to be enwrapped by divine light, who longs to live with truth, gratitude, and love. Hands that are empty are filled by the faithful God, rich with goodness and with mercy. Blessings lead people of prayer and faith to Christ, so that Christ might be in our hearts every day and so that we might live in the benevolence of the Father.

The gesture of blessing offers the certainty that God cares for the believers from the very beginning of the day, enriching us with God's power and accompanying us during our journeys. God's presence lives in us, so that we may follow the cross of Christ, in which there is salvation, life, and redemption.

20

Eating and Drinking

Eating and drinking, the most common gestures of the human condition, assume a particular meaning when they are experienced in community. In fact, eating and drinking with others express a profound sense of communion. When sharing food or drink, people feel united and discuss their concerns and ideals. Food and drink speak of the complete nourishment of the human being and symbolize the community of those who dine together.

In both concrete and figurative language of eating and drinking, we express a desire for union, of being one for others, of being of one heart and spirit. People who are not at peace, who are split apart or angry, do not want to sit at a common table and share the same meal. The vocation of living in peace is a gift the Creator has planted in the heart of every creature and that is evident in everyday life.

When we gather to eat and drink together, we certify that this very action is more important than the food and drink itself. The joy of being with others in this setting is what is most important. One who centers attention on the food has a misplaced center of interest. The more simple the meal, the more it is possible to emphasize the values of sharing, familiarity, and fraternity.

Usually eating and drinking together is preceded by an invitation, and the one who offers the invitation gives evidence of the desire to share significantly with the guests. The invitation comes from the desire to see friendship mature. In giving and in accepting invitations we move away from solitariness and toward forming a single heart and spirit. In eating and drinking together we form interpersonal relationships, bonding, and harmony.

When Jesus said to us: "Take and eat. . . . Take and drink," he wanted to enter an intimate relationship with us. The Master always invites us to the eucharistic banquet so that we may one day be enriched at the heavenly banquet. It is not we who draw ourselves near the eucharistic gifts but the Lord who invites us to his passover, who leads us to his ideals. He wants to remain with us and to have us remain in him. The joy of reciprocity in the "now" of the Father is the relationship that Jesus offers us through faith and through the sacraments.

Our following the Gospel can be diverted by sin, by not adhering to the divine truths, and by not following the Easter and Pentecost events. Christ Jesus longs to share his passover with us, to communicate his divine presence to us, and to have us realize that our salvation is through him.

When in the Spirit we are together at the eucharistic meal, we have the joy of sharing the true meaning of existence, that meaning that Christ lived and that animated every moment of his life: the offering of self into the hands of the Father for the joy and salvation of humanity. Sharing this attitude, we will grow in divine and sacramental communion, in expectation of an eternal communion.

The joy of eating and drinking with the Lord becomes in its way the source of our Christian witness, as the apostle Peter teaches us in his discourse at the house of Cornelius: "But God raised him on the third day and allowed him to appear, not to all the people but to us who were chosen by God as witnesses, and who ate and drank with him after he rose from the dead" (Acts 10:40-41). The love that animates the church lives from the common eucharistic experience, in which we become one single person in the Lord and which provides in our daily lives a community of life with the Father.

Eating and drinking with Jesus is where we rejoice in the certainty of entering into communion with him who is truly present in our lives as the resurrected one and whom we never have to fear. In the Eucharist we see the Lord. Like the disciples at Emmaus, we recognize him in the breaking of the bread. Our eating and drinking does not reduce itself to a simple process of taking in food. Rather, it is rooted in a pilgrimage of communion that is a sharing, seeing, and communicating with the mystery of Easter: Christ dead and resurrected, who is always present in his church to lead it to the kingdom.

Incensing

St. Paul bid the Romans to follow the new life of Christ and to present themselves as "a living sacrifice, holy and acceptable to God, which is your spiritual worship" (Rom 12:1). The use of incense reminds us of this vocation that is proper to every disciple of the Redeemer. Incense in the liturgy expresses the offertory posture of the community and reflects that the prayer of the community arises from the fullness of their hearts. That which appears externally expresses the heart of the offering one.

The psalmist presents incense as an expression of the intensity of his life: "I call upon you, O LORD; come quickly to me; / give ear to my voice when I call to you. / Let my prayer be counted as incense before you, / and the lifting up of my hands as an evening sacrifice" (Ps 141:1-2).

The book of Revelation reminds us that the prayer of the saints is like the scent that emerges from the censer: "Another angel with a golden censer came and stood at the altar; he was given a great quantity of incense to offer with the prayers of all the saints on the golden altar that is before the throne. And the smoke of the incense, with the prayers of the saints, rose before God from the hand of the angel" (Rev 8:3-4).

The rising of this scent is the soul moving toward God. It is the very meaning of our existence; it is the turning of our hearts to the Absolute. While our bodies are physically linked to the earth, we cannot remain prisoners of the concrete. Like incense we move toward the heights; we long incessantly to meet God face to face. "As a deer longs for flowing streams, / so my soul longs for you, O God. / My soul thirsts for God, / for the living God. / When shall I come and behold / the face of God?" (Ps 42:1-2). The gesture of raising the censer from which the incense escapes is not a simple, planned gesture; rather, it is a ritual that reflects our inner self: "To you, O LORD, I lift up my soul" (Ps 25:1). The smoking censer is prayer in action; it is an ineffable melody of supplication and praise presented to the Most High. It expresses the love and abandonment of the community to God.

The spiritual attitude expressed by the incense gives significance to the environment in which it is offered. The smoke and the scent of the incense enwrap the place in which we worship and remind us how for the Hebrews the cloud of the glory of God was the place where the people talked with God, who dwelt in his sanctuary: "When Moses entered the tent, the pillar of cloud would descend and stand at the entrance of the tent, and the LORD would speak with Moses" (Exod 33:9). "And when the priests came out of the holy place, a cloud filled the house of the LORD, . . . for the glory of the LORD filled the house of the LORD" (1 Kgs 8:10-11).

Ritual is never a simple gesture that the community engages in mechanically. Ritual comes alive from the participation of those present. Incense reminds the faithful that they are in the presence of the Most High, surrounded by the perfume and the cloud of the burning incense. The liturgical assembly has an atmosphere of sacrifice and praise. The incense helps place us in a sacrificial posture, making our own the offering of Christ to the Father.

The *General Instruction of the Roman Missal* regarding the use of incense during the Mass affirms that "The priest may incense the gifts placed upon the altar and then incense the cross and the altar itself, so as to signify the Church's offering and prayer rising like incense in the sight of God. Next, the priest, because of his sacred ministry, and the people, by reason of their baptismal dignity, may be incensed by the deacon or another minister" (75).

The scent that arises from the incense indicates the giving of our total self into the hands of God in imitation of the attitude of Christ, who in the sign of the bread and wine is a living offering to the Father for the redemption of humanity.

The use of incense in the celebration of Lauds and Vespers underlines once again this offering and sacrificial dimension of prayer, which is like incense rising to God. The incense that accompanies the singing of the *Benedictus* and the *Magnificat* expresses how the praying community places itself before God in a pleasing sacrifice. The entire day, therefore, between the moments of prayer in the morning and the evening and at whose center stands the eucharistic celebration, is a true sacrificial and eucharistic act to the Most High.

The use of incense also signifies the value of purification. As perfume drives away unpleasant odors, so incense drives away the power of evil. When we present our offerings, we should be pure of heart. The incensing of persons and of places underlines this meaning, and it creates in the celebrants the consciousness of needing to place themselves in communion with God, so that the sacrifice of their lives may be pleasing and acceptable to God.

The incensing of the celebrant thus becomes particularly important in that it points to the meaning of the celebrant's presence in the midst of the assembly. The celebrant acts in the person of Christ, in service of the gathered community. Thus while receiving honor symbolized by the incensing, the celebrant must remember to be in imitation of Christ in this posture of offering. The assembly, for its part, is offered with Jesus and with the celebrant.

And last, the church incenses the bodies of our dead brothers and sisters to honor the temple of those who have been called to eternity. That body is the reliquary of the indwelling of the Most Holy Trinity and of one who was created in the image and likeness of God. The church may do nothing less than honor that body in professing its faith in the wonders of God who has created us.

22

Presenting the Gifts

Every religion offers prayers and sacrifices in rituals that express the needs of the community and its faith experience in relationship to God. In the liturgy of our eucharistic celebrations the presentation of the gifts follows the style of the Old Testament in which the firstfruits of the harvest were offered to God: "It is praiseworthy for the bread and wine to be presented by the faithful. . . . It is well also that money or other gifts for the poor or for the Church, brought by the faithful or collected in the church, should be received" (*General Instruction of the Roman Missal* 73).

Every gesture of the celebration expresses the intention of the community. The processional rite of the presentation of the gifts recognizes that everything that is offered is a gift from God. The baptized approach God offering the firstfruits of the earth, so that those gifts may be the source of the eucharistic bread and wine. The other offerings also identify with the needs of the community. Such a posture of offering to God and with our brothers and sisters helps every member of the Christian community overcome the temptation of being too possessive about things, as if we were the owners of such things.

What the earth produces because of our labor is a gift from God. We express our sense of gratitude to God in the presentation of the gifts; we give back to God what God has first given to us. That presentation of the gifts is a profession of faith in action where we pray and sing our gratitude to the Creator. We rejoice for the opportunity to give back to God what we have received from God. In the heart of every celebrant there vibrates the joy of the gift and gratitude to the one who is the source of every created reality, the joy of being able to give back that which has been received from the hands of the Giver of every good thing.

In the presentation of the gifts we celebrate that God is Creator, Redeemer, Lord. This attitude is particularly important in the context of the eucharistic celebration. The liturgy resounds with gratitude for the wonders that God has provided us in our creation and redemption. The presentation of the gifts also points to our being enriched in every moment by God. In presenting to God that which God has given freely, the community lives its conviction that God will also be with us in the future. Every thank you given to the Most High is the beginning of new grace and renewed communion.

In bringing the gifts we express familiarity with God before the altar. Presenting the gifts is a sign of the community's gratitude to the Father and to the one and triune God. Gratitude is not simply an offering of something but underlines that the person lives in communion with the divine giver and shares that giver's joy in self-giving. Reciprocity thus animates the sign of bringing the gifts to the altar. Communion is strengthened, and we receive God's blessing. And the gifts that are transformed become a sign of the sacrificing will of Christ on the cross.

God in his plan of salvation wishes us to use the gifts of the earth to bring joy to our hearts and to share these gifts with our brothers and sisters. The presentation of the gifts expresses our wish to share goods with others. God accepts the gifts in order to redistribute them. Everything that we give to God reflects God's communion with us.

True joy follows upon every gesture of offering. The joy of giving does not derive from privation but from the building of communion. The privation of the "I" becomes the richness of the "we." The presentation of the gifts thus becomes a means of shared liberty and a sign of unity and reciprocity with each other according to the wishes of the Father.

The experience of the apostolic church teaches us that "the whole group of those who believed were of one heart and soul, and no one claimed private ownership of any possessions, but everything they owned was held in common. . . . There was not a needy person among them, for as many as owned lands or houses sold them and brought the proceeds of what was sold. They laid it at the apostles' feet, and it was distributed to each as any had need" (Acts 4:32-35).

The liturgy parallels the gestures of every day. Every instant is a grace. Every instant lived in fullness is an act of gratitude. Every instant is one to give again as a gift. Every instant is an opportunity for fraternity. The liturgy is born from life. The community thus becomes prepared to participate in the eucharistic offering where Christ does not offer us material things but his very self, and in offering himself gives birth to a communion of humanity.

23

Lighting

The Easter Vigil is a passage from shadow into light. The presence in the assembly of the illuminated paschal candle that spreads its glimmer into the darkness of that holy night is a sign of the Resurrected One who appears in the midst of his own. The prayer of the church says to us: "May the light of Christ, rising in glory, / dispel the darkness of our hearts and minds."

Christ is the light of the world: "I am the light of the world. Whoever follows me will never walk in darkness but will have the light of life" (John 8:12).

To light a candle is to proclaim this faith. By means of our Christian choice, the shadows of sin are defeated and the assembly is enwrapped in the light by pure grace. The presence of the paschal candle in the assembly until Pentecost is a living hymn to the mystery of the resurrection. It signifies that the presence of the glorified Master may always be firmly rooted among us. That which happened on one night extends itself in time.

This gesture, solemnized in the vigil and in the Easter season, lives from the hope that is present in the heart of every person not to be overcome by shadows but rather to live at peace with his or her brothers and sisters. The lighting of any light for overcoming darkness is a simple but powerful statement that reminds us that we were not made for death but for life, and that the soul should wake up again from sluggishness. The apostle Paul reminds us: "Sleeper, awake! / Rise from the dead, / and Christ will shine on you" (Eph 5:14).

Light suggests energy, a will to live, a desire for fullness and communion, the overcoming of stagnation or coldness. That tiny flame, while it floods its surroundings with light, speaks of heat, of the force of life, of overcoming solitude, of the vitality and the worth of things, of the pilgrimage of life notwithstanding the difficulties we face in our daily lives. Everything thus becomes a sign of the transcendent that surrounds us and emphasizes the victory of light over darkness. There is a strict relation between light and heat, between seeing and understanding, between being the light of Christ and the fire of divine love. In this perspective the church thus prays in the prayer after Communion in the Common of Saints: "O God, present and operative in all your sacraments, illumine and enflame our own spirit."

The power of the Spirit is invoked as the church prays on Pentecost in the opening prayer of the eucharistic celebration: "God our Father, / let the Spirit you sent on your Church / to begin the teaching of the gospel / continue to work in the world / through the hearts of all who believe." Seen through the lens of the mystery of Christ, the lighting of a candle makes a multiplicity of sentiments echo in the soul, sentiments with one common element: the joy of living and of new life.

The presence of a lit candle encourages us to pray. Sometimes when prayer is not possible, we might light a candle so that our desire for prayer and supplication may always be present in our lives. In this light that burns there is the desire of a praying heart to be elevated, a heart consumed by faithfulness to God. As in the Easter Vigil, the lit candle is an expression of the prayer of the community bringing to life amid darkness the faithfulness of the Father who never deludes. Lighting a candle gives witness to our desire for prayer. Every lit candle is a hymn to life from the praying heart that lives from the God who never disappoints.

This climate of faith and prayer is manifested in celebrative language in baptism. The parent of the one to be baptized lights a candle from the Easter candle, so that the gift of faith in Christ dead and risen may never be extinguished in the heart of the child. The light is given so that the child may meet the Lord when the Lord comes in glory, a reference here to the beautiful image of the parable of the bridesmaids (cf. Matt 25:1-13). The light that has been lit is an acceptance of salvation and a desire to grow in this salvation to the joy of the final coming of the Redeemer.

In the rite of baptism the parent, holding the lit candle to illuminate the child, proclaims the task of leading the newly baptized to the passover of the Lord, so that the child may always walk joyfully in the light of Christ.

To light a candle is a choice of life. Only the Master may illuminate our hearts. He is the companion for our journey, the one who gives light to our life. We light our lamps in processions in order to affirm before the world that Christ alone, with his light, gives meaning to human existence. Our walking in the light is based in our being children of the light, as Paul says to us: "the night is far gone, the day is near. Let us then lay aside the works of darkness and put on the armor of light; let us live honorably as in the day, . . . Instead, put on the Lord Jesus Christ" (Rom 13:12-14).

That lit candle that gives light to the processional walk of the community reveals how Jesus will illuminate the hearts of believers and cast away all shadows. The act of lighting the candle is an act of living faith. It is a living desire to be in the light and destroy the darkness that kills the soul. In this gesture we proclaim the triumph of Christ over the powers of evil, and we give witness to the desire for life that is present in the heart of every person. In this we say that the hope necessary for our walk through life comes from on high. We will ourselves be a candle that remains unlit, unless we approach the light that gives life to us.

To light a candle is a sign that God offers us the capacity to let the power of the Most High shine before all the world. That candle is a sign of the mystery of the incarnation that the Spirit enlivens in us. In every moment we offer ourselves to God so that God will send the Spirit to light in us the fire of divine love, a love which can give to our life that heat and that light that enable us to walk our way through time.

Thus to light a candle expresses our conviction that Christ illuminates our whole person so that we may walk in hope, waiting for the day that will know no sunset.

24

Presiding

In our liturgical assemblies, in remembering our baptismal vocation, we gather in the Lord to become ever more people of the Lord. In this pursuit we are not left to ourselves. Rather, we are guided by a brother in the faith, usually a priest, who presides in the various sacramental celebrations. This leadership, which we see every time we gather in the name of the Lord, is signified by the presence of the chair of the celebrant in the sanctuary. The *General Instruction of the Roman Missal* puts it this way: "The chair of the priest celebrant must signify his office of presiding over the gathering and of directing the prayer. Thus the best place for the chair is in a position facing the people at the head of the sanctuary, unless the design of the building or other circumstances impede this: for example, if the great distance would interfere with communication between the priest and the gathered assembly" (310). Both the person of the presider and the environment of the assembly are important in presiding over an assembly convoked in faith, hope, and love.

The presider takes his place in front of the assembly, not so much to indicate authority but rather as a sign of the event that gathers the assembly. The gift of presiding exists in persons who know themselves to be elected, or called to preside. Every gathering takes place under a presider, so that all gatherings may achieve in an orderly way the tasks proper to them. This presidential structure is contingent and transitory, but in the sacramental order its significance is in the synthesis of history and mystery. The principle that animates the congregation is bringing the message of eternal life to the people. All of us gather in the assembly in obedience to the Spirit. In the ordained minister there is signified the presence of Christ in the midst of his own, according to the promise made to the disciples: "For where two or three are gathered in my name, I am there among them" (Matt 18:20). "I am with you always, to the end of the age" (Matt 28:20). The ecclesial convocation in the assembly lives this affirmation of faith: Christ is Lord.

No truth may remain abstract, since it must be understood by the faithful. In the Gospel perspective the tradition has given us the sacramental sign to signify the action of Christ, who gathers into his presence the whole assembly and defines the assembly with his being and action. Christ in his sacramental presence convokes, gathers, gives his word, places the sacramental signs, dismisses us, and sends us out again into the world. Ministry, especially that of the ordained, brings this reality to light. Conscious of his own particular duty, the one who is deputized by the Spirit to preside is called to educate the community to the divine presence, to an acceptance of the salvation that comes from on high, and to a sense of the sacred. The reign of God is in the midst of God's own. The joy of the assembly matures the presider, who with the Spirit—during the celebration and by means of his actions, words, and posture—proclaims that great events are happening, that he and his brothers and sisters in the assembly are gathered in the presence of God.

The presider is a sign of the presence of the Christ who communicates his passover to those gathered in faith, gathered for their regeneration. The presider is not only in a physically more elevated position with respect to the assembly but he also stands before his brothers and sisters in the new exodus, in order to lead them to the Promised Land. This sacramental presidency lives from the vitality of the people of God, who every day are on a pilgrimage by means of their baptism. The presider gathers the assembly in the name of the Trinity to proclaim the word and to witness the paschal event in the eucharistic prayer, so that the people of God may not tire of being called into the light that comes from on high.

The presider by living again the sentiments and ideals of Christ develops the communion of the assembly. His ministry has nothing to do with authoritarianism but lives from the attitude of the Master, the true Lord of the assembly, who came into the world not to be served by it but to serve and to give his life in ransom for the many. Similarly, the presider is called to communicate, to favor, and to develop the gift of unity that represents the Easter message. The presider must be open to the Spirit working within the assembly, as happened on the first Pentecost with the first faithful who "devoted themselves to the apostles' teaching and fellowship, to the breaking of bread and the prayers" (Acts 2:42).

The sign of the ministry of the presider thus represents a continually new call to the faithful, who, when they are gathered in the assembly, are regenerated from on high and are led toward the fullness of salvation. They live with their faces turned toward the cross, because only from that tree does salvation flow, a salvation that makes us a communion with and a source of hope for humanity.

25

Bowing

The eucharistic celebration ritual opens with the gesture of the ministers who, approaching the altar with a bow, place themselves in a state of veneration. This posture has a double value: it explains

1. the understanding of being in the presence of the loving oblation of Christ in the incarnate paschal sign of the altar, sublime mystery that fascinates humankind;

2. the hope of realizing a journey of communion/identification with the Teacher. The church through this gesture wants to help the assembly to intuit the necessity of undergoing an intense internal development so that the event of salvation might become the hinge in the life of everyone. We are called as creatures to place ourselves before Christ, to be in Christ and as Christ a living sacrifice, holy and pleasing to the Father. Such a spiritual experience is revived by the celebrant in the unfolding of the liturgical action before the altar. This action invites the faithful to feel themselves called around the altar of the Lord, a sign of his salvific presence that is at work in all who, in his resurrection, rediscover the foundation of their history. This is underscored in a particular manner on Sunday and on occasions of solemn celebrations, in the act of proclaiming the "creed" with which every Christian makes the profession of faith and chooses the faith.

In the gesture of bowing the head during the proclamation of the sign/creed, one reinterprets the consciousness that is the foundation of the believers' existence in the history of Jesus. In the bowing of the head at the words, "by the power of the Holy Spirit / he was born of the Virgin Mary, and became man," the assembly identifies itself in the annihilation of the Word in order to be able to enter into the exaltation of the paschal mystery with an upright bodily position (cf. Phil 2:6-11).

In the form of each liturgical action, every bow recalls this paschal vitality and stimulates the celebrants to always penetrate deeper into the feelings of the Master through the concrete means of corporal actions.

It is understood in this light, then, that the deep bowing of the head in the celebration of the Liturgy of the Hours proclaims at the doxology "Glory to the Father, and to the Son, and to the Holy Spirit" or similar. The hymns and the psalms translate the fecundity of the history of salvation that proceeds from the principle actors: the Father, in the Son, through the work of the Holy Spirit. The exultant knowledge of their renewing presence causes the assembly to bow in the contemplation of the Trinity during the final doxology.

The persons who allow themselves to become involved in the history of God, with the profound faith supported by the gesture of bowing the head and the whole person, give praise with contemplative emotion to the life of the three Divine Persons, in a way that is similar to the four living creatures and the twenty-four elders who in the exultant liturgy in the book of Revelation sing a new song (5:9) and prostrate themselves in adoration (5:14). Every liturgy is conferred in contemplative style and grafts itself to the economy of salvation; thus in the prayerful bow we share in a "shipwrecked" love in the life of the Divine Persons in order to enjoy the fruitful beauty of trinitarian love.

At the historical/salvific base of the bow, the figure of the celebrant takes shape: a creature who, in his poverty, is called to the mission to announce the paschal wonders of the Father.

The deacon, first to proclaim the Gospel, bows before the presider of the liturgical assembly to receive the benediction that will allow him to assume this role. The cleric, when he stands ready to give voice to the Gospel, bows before the altar and says softly, "Almighty God, cleanse my heart and my lips that I may worthily proclaim your gospel." In both ministers is understood the profound meaning of the first limitations before the mission of incarnating the person of the Risen One who continues to nourish the hope in the ecclesiastical community, to resonate the word of salvation.

Again the presbyter, during the proclamation of Eucharistic Prayer I (The Roman Canon), at the moment of the offering ("Almighty God, / we pray that your angel may take this sacrifice / to your altar in heaven"), bows with his hands joined as evidence of his posture of humility in offering the eucharistic gifts to the Father, and so indicates the fruitfulness of the offering by concluding the prayer, standing erect, and making the sign of the cross. On he who bows in the presence of the Father the offering of the Son descends, through pure divine condescension, the fullness of "every grace and blessing" in heaven. In this dynamism is concretized the evangelical principle: "For all who exalt themselves will be humbled, and those who humble themselves will be exalted" (Luke 14:11). The bow educates every celebrant to mature in Gospel humility. Thus it is in this posture that the three Divine Persons work wonders and invite every disciple into trinitarian communion.

At the conclusion of the solemn blessings, the deacon turns to the assembly, saying, "Bow your heads and pray for God's blessing." This posture of the body indicates the will to model one's being into a constant availability to the mystery of Christ in a condition of openness to the graciousness of God and to his divine power. The assembly, recognizing its unworthiness before the eucharistic will of Christ who invites the disciples to be living and believable signs of the new world, places itself in an active posture of supplication, because God continues to work in its history. The people of the assembly know spiritually they must relive the experience of the apostles in the first years of the Christian community, according to the description of the evangelist Mark in specifying their mission: "And they went out and proclaimed the good news everywhere, while the Lord worked with them and confirmed the message by the signs that accompanied it" (Mark 16:20).

The bow explains the invocation of "poverty of spirit" that is present in the posture of welcoming of the gift of salvation, in the desire that the Father make a new person of every celebrant. It is the gesture that explains the consciousness that one cannot stand or hide before the divine presence without opening oneself to the invading power that comes from on high.

With the successive judgment of the body, the celebrants explain the conviction that the supplication has been exhausted and that effective fulfillment of the salvific event has been given. In daily existence the disciple therefore places himself in the daily condition of openness, so that the personal posture of all creatures always reflects in salvation history a glorious transparency of the faithfulness of the Father in the pain of each day.

26

Exchange of Peace

In the context of the communion rite of the Roman liturgy there is an invitation to give a clear immediate gesture of an exchange of peace. The priest (or deacon) addresses the assembly with the invitation: "Let us offer each other a sign of peace" (or a similar formula, which is suggested in the Sacramentary). To understand this rite, it is important that we become familiar with the liturgical text. The premises of the Roman Missal say thus: "The Rite of Peace follows, by which the Church asks for peace and unity for herself and for the whole human family, and the faithful express to each other their ecclesial communion and mutual charity before communicating in the Sacrament. As for the sign of peace to be given, the manner is to be established by the Conferences of Bishops in accordance with the culture and customs of the peoples" (*General Instruction of the Roman Missal* 82). Every ritual gesture finds its explanation in the Scriptures and has the purpose, on one hand, to make the action more real, and on the other hand, to overcome the risk of being considered a daily routine.

The gesture of the exchange of peace is understood in the fabric of the entire celebration and is founded on the reports of post-paschal apparitions of the risen Christ. The community in this particular celebrative moment is directed to enter into the gesture of Jesus who broke the bread with his disciples in order to share with them the mystery of his death and resurrection. According to the narrative style of the evangelists (cf. Luke 24:36; John 20:19), the risen Lord appeared to his own and communicated to them the new life springing forth from his resurrection: the messianic peace promised at the Last Supper (cf. John 14:27). The prayer that, in the liturgy, precedes the exchange of peace, brings us into this event ("Lord Jesus Christ, you said to your apostles: 'I leave you peace, my peace I give you'") and strengthens us in the conviction that the Lord is giving us the gift of his peace ("The peace of the Lord be with you always"). The exchange of peace draws meaning from the sacramental presence of the Risen because the faithful share the Spirit in such a way as to generate fraternal communion according to the Gospel model. It is Christ who gives life to the invisible bond that unites the brothers and sisters in the faith and makes them one body and one Spirit. Only in such a fraternal fashion can the eucharistic gifts become fruitful. As a result, the paschal mystery, which gives life, is placed in our hearts and is the extension of a universal embrace to all humanity. Thus in that moment, that particular eucharistic assembly is present and all humanity is in evangelical communion. One understands, then, the tight relationship between the beginning of the eucharistic celebration in which the risen Lord gives us his peace, and the gesture of communion with which, in the exaltation of the Spirit, we enjoy the profound paschal significance of being together to receive the gifts of "body given" and of "blood shed." In such a way, the New Testament canticle that the apostle Paul offers in the letter to the Ephesians is made visible: "But now in Christ Jesus you who once were far off have been brought near by the blood of Christ. For he is our peace; in his flesh he has made both groups into one" (Eph 2:13-14).

The sharing of the dominion of Christ is understood through methods that manifest a true and fruitful experience of communion: the kiss of peace, the handshake, the fraternal embrace, or other gestures that different cultures have developed over time. This celebrative expression has its roots in the New Testament tradition. The intention of the exchange of a fraternal kiss is suggested by the apostle Paul: "Brothers and sisters, farewell. Put things in order, listen to my appeal, agree with one another, live in peace; and the God of love and peace will be with you. Greet one another with a holy kiss. All the saints greet you" (2 Cor 13:11-12). The kiss is a sign of the mystery of communion that unites the celebrants, who are, in fact, the saints (cf. 2 Cor 1:1). It explains, communicates, and shares the significance that animates the life of the community that stands celebrating the divine mysteries. In this is evidenced the elation of the communal belonging to the Most Holy Trinity (cf. 2 Cor 13:13) and the exultation of communicating such interior life to the brothers and sisters in such a way that together they grow in the divine intimacy that is ready to be offered in the eucharistic gifts. The "kiss of the communion among the saints" opens the door to the premise of "holy gifts" because of the reciprocity among the disciples who are in Christ and in the Holy Spirit. The truth of the eucharistic communion appears with all of its force if the disciples live the joy of being one in each other, according to the beautiful image of the vine and the branches (cf. John 15:1-5) and the invitation of Jesus directed to the disciples because they are his authentic imitators (cf. John 13:15-16). Also, the second gesture, traditionally the extending of the hand, is characterized by the profound nature of its reciprocal nature, if we can understand the more profound significance of it.

The hand possesses its own vitality, thus it explains the richness of the interior life of a person. In the gesture of two persons shaking hands we see the communication of a spiritual experience that characterizes the two personalities. A hand joined with another hand indicates the initial fruitfulness of an intense interpersonal reciprocity seen in the prospective of a marked dialogue that comes from a strong effective component. This demonstrates the relational development of persons who want to share the same meaning of life. The context, then, that surrounds and qualifies such gestures, ultimately defines the sense of reciprocity. The ambience of the celebration is understood by the presence of the risen Lord who not only is present in the eucharistic assembly but also is accomplishing a renewal in the person of each member of the eucharistic celebration. In the exchange of peace, through the stretching out of the hand, the assembly breathes the creative communion of the Holy Spirit and illuminates the fact that people love to give themselves to their brothers or sisters in Christ Jesus and bring together their brothers and sisters as Christ himself did. The seriousness placed on these gestures redefines that intense climate of prayer that animates the celebrants and that introduces them to the trinitarian communion in a way that makes real the principle of the epiclesis of communion: "Grant that we, who are nourished by his body and blood, may be filled with his Holy Spirit, and become one body, one spirit in Christ." The gesture indicates an intense and fruitful relationship between Christ and his own, an unequal relationship in which God communicates himself to humanity, and humanity, animated by an exalted recognition in the face of the free generosity of the Master, is able to accept it in the eucharistic gifts. This is also the sense of the sign of embracing, which communicates the firm desire to become one person in a peace that comes from Christ's death and resurrection and that gives the gesture the ability to form an ecclesiastical fraternity in the gift of the Holy Spirit. Thus is explained through the senses the tension of that unity in Christ, which is dynamism brought forth from the eucharistic celebration.

The gift that the eucharistic prayer offers to the celebrating community can only be assumed if the ones who are preparing to accept the Master, dead and risen in the eucharistic signs, live intensely the theological life of a strong communion in the paschal mystery of Jesus and in the Pentecost of the Holy Spirit. Such experience educates the disciples to live and to share the "invisible" gift of salvation by means of the form of sacramental gestures.

27

Breaking the Bread

The eucharistic mystery has assumed in the New Testament tradition the term "breaking of bread" (cf. Luke 24:30; Acts 2:42; 20:7), which helps uncover in this particular aspect of the sacramental event its own particular significance for the entire rite. It is important to point out that it is in the atmosphere of the whole rite of communion that we find the action of the breaking of the bread, which helps the disciples understand how the gift of receiving the eucharistic gifts must generate a communion, a condition where they know to draw near to the "mystical-sacramental" sense of the ritual act. As is explained in the Roman Missal: "Christ's gesture of breaking bread at the Last Supper, which gave the entire Eucharistic Action its name in apostolic times, signifies that the many faithful are made one body (1 Cor 10:17) by receiving Communion from the one Bread of Life which is Christ, who died and rose for the salvation of the world" (*General Instruction of the Roman Missal* 83).

This spiritual experience is redefined in the breaking of the one bread into small fragments to be shared with the brothers and sisters in the faith. The more profound significance of this rite is ultimately seen when one of the pieces is placed in the chalice in the context of the invocation/acclamation: "Lamb of God, you take away the sins of the world." This act is then understood in the context of the eucharistic gifts from the priest and ministers and the distribution of communion to the faithful. This connection helps us clearly intuit that the value of the action of the breaking of the bread gives entitlement to the people of the liturgical assembly who stand ready to open themselves up to the gifts of eucharistic bread and wine.

Here we enter into a ritualistic itinerary that reinterprets the spiritual journey of the celebrating community. On the altar is placed the one bread, Jesus Christ, who wishes to draw everyone into himself in communion with the Father. We uncover then the path that the eucharistic mystery offers to us in our everyday life: from the life of the Trinity, culminating in the Pasch of Jesus, springs forth the action of the breaking of the bread and then taking it. The whole history of the disciple lives and is oriented toward this communion, a mystery that revolves within the person of Jesus dead and risen. If the proclamation of the eucharistic prayer introduced the celebrating assembly into the history of salvation, then the ritualization that characterizes communion must represent its actualization.

Singing the "Lamb of God" creates an oblative atmosphere of the cross. Here Christ, the new Lamb of God, dies in order to join into one the children scattered abroad (cf. John 11:52), drawing all to himself (cf. John 12:32). It is a fascinating aspect of this mystery of communion that surrounds the disciples who orient their gaze "on the one whom they have pierced" (cf. John 19:37). The action of breaking the bread explains the desire of the Teacher that every person live in communion with the Father, as Jesus himself prayed at the Last Supper: "for their sakes I sanctify myself, so that they also may be sanctified in truth" (cf. John 17:19). The action that in the first place seems to follow an immediate function, which is the distribution of the eucharistic bread to all the faithful, then takes on a more profound mystical and spiritual significance when penetrated and reread in a theological and believing way. One cannot receive communion if one doesn't become one with Christ's body given up and blood poured out. This profound value is recalled by the celebrant when he places a small fragment of the broken host into the chalice. Originally, this action evidenced the gift of communion with the one eucharistic mystery of the Bishop of Rome, who wished to "regulate" the eucharistic communion by the priests who celebrated in other liturgical assemblies. On the theological and spiritual front this action assumes a much greater significance, for the edification of a community that wishes to call itself eucharistic.

The bread in its very essence is an intense experience of communion: the many grains of wheat become one loaf of bread. It is a sign of Christ who brings together around himself all humanity, forming them into a unity through his sacrificial love (cf. *Didache* X). They become one liturgical assembly that, reunited around the one altar of the Lord, shares the same bread, a surprising mystery of communion (cf. 1 Cor 10:16). Such a vocation finds its truth in the mystery of the offering that Jesus made of himself on Calvary through the effusion of his own blood (cf. Heb 9:14, 28; 10:10). In placing the fragment of bread in the chalice, the priest begins a very simple process: the wine itself soaks the fragment of bread. Herein we grasp the profundity of the mystery. The Eucharist is clearly the living face of the vocation to communion that characterizes the Christian community (cf. John 17:22). Nevertheless, such an event cannot be fruitful to the whole community if not realized in the context of its existence as an oblation in theological, sacramental, and existential "imitate on" of Christ who, in his blood poured out, bore the unification of humanity within himself (cf. Col 1:20; Eph 1:10). And in his person, given in the freedom of love and of communion, illuminates the history of every person. True fraternal sharing cannot take place if love does not become a gift in itself for every person, that is, if one does not live in the sacrificial heart of the Master. Thus it is possible to see within the mystery how the offering of one's life becomes a part of Christ's own fruitful life of communion of the community and gives it salvific significance. Christians, in chanting the Lamb of God, allow themselves to become involved in the contemplation of the Crucified One from whom flowed blood and water, and learn to love their history as incarnations of the offering of the Master so as to create a communion procession. So, as the Father thought it, Jesus built it, and the Holy Spirit brought it to completion in the efficacy of redemption. In that chalice, in the force of the created power of the Holy Spirit, the unity of the person of Christ is "reconstituted": the body given and the blood poured out in the Holy Spirit becomes Christ himself in his fullness, as a gift to all humanity. In the chalice then, all disciples of the Lord rediscover the fountain and spirit of their existence as disciples: they are called to accomplish in themselves the Pasch of the Master in order to mature in trinitarian communion.

The act, then, of receiving the gifts of bread and wine reinterprets the firm will of the disciple to enliven the everyday decisions in life in light of the mystery that is present in the eucharistic gifts. In fact, Christ's body given up and his blood poured out penetrate into all disciples, giving life to their existential faculties and potentialities and directing the disciples to become the living heart of Christ in the daily journey of life. Only in this way can the ritualistic action become not only an expression of a profession of faith in the paschal mystery but also the reference point to elaborate a relationship among brothers and sisters that is only illuminated from the one who on the cross drew all human creatures to himself. Those who approach the eucharistic gifts must feel themselves involved in the communal and sacrificial mystery of the breaking of the bread in order to make real the will to open themselves up to the person of the risen Christ. In that Amen, which baptized persons profess when the priest gives them the eucharistic gifts—"The body of Christ. The blood of Christ"—they are rooted in the joy of wanting to make their own life stories imitations of the living Christ, through a growing passion for fraternal communion, in the image of the circle of love that is the life of the three Divine Persons. The mystery that is "sung" during the eucharistic prayer is assumed in the eucharistic gifts of communion because all those celebrating discover their proper identities in the paschal fruitfulness of the Teacher and understand that true unity is not possible without letting go in order to dedicate oneself to the Father and to all humanity. Those who share the body given and the blood poured out feel, therefore, the urgency in themselves to become "in" Christ and "as" Christ, body given and blood poured out with and for their brothers and sisters so as to expand the sense of the eucharistic celebration: that all people might become one reality in the imitation of the communion that exists between the Father and the Son.

28

Entering into Church

The Holy Spirit works in the heart of all Christians and regenerates them by stimulating them to long for the true experience of communion with the Teacher and with their brothers and sisters. The church, through the liturgical assembly, is the sign of this constant vocation of proceeding in communion.

For the disciple of the Lord, therefore, the desire to enter the hall of the liturgical celebration constitutes a normal experience, one could say, but this brings with it the risk of not understanding all the richness and freshness, and not having an intense attitude of oneness and wonder, of acceptance and of development of the gift of conversion. Every liturgical celebration incarnates a style of life, translating the dynamic action in the hearts of the believers who hear within themselves the invitation of the Master: "Come to me, all you that are weary and are carrying heavy burdens, and I will give you rest" (Matt 11:28). It is possible to respond to the call only in one way: leave one's house, one's particular ways and activities, in order to follow Christ who is the true and one light that illuminates the way for every creature (cf. John 8:12). Disciples feel invited every week to make personal Christ's initiative, which they pull into themselves because they desire Christ to make his dwelling in divine-human intimacy within them. The sound of the bell itself becomes the actualization of the word of Christ, always present, which still today guides us with all of its charismatic force: "Follow me, leave everything, allow me to live my resurrection in you, in order for you to celebrate with me the day of your freedom in the heavenly kingdom." In fact, it is important to rediscover the sense of the sound of the bell, as the blessing rite of the bells teaches us in its promises: "It is an ancient practice to summon the Christian people to the liturgical assembly by means of some sign or signal and also to alert them to important happenings in the local community. The peal of bells, then, is in a way the expression of the sentiments of the people of God as they rejoice or grieve, offer thanks or petition, gather together and show outwardly the mystery of their oneness in Christ" (*Book of Blessings* 1305). In this vision we can understand our procession into church as a continuation of the actuality of the catechumenal journey that allows us to celebrate the ritual in spirit and in truth, and thus identifies us with Jesus, our Teacher and our Lord. We hear the voice that tells us, "Come, and see; you will be with me, and you will enjoy my glory. You will enter into communion with the Father, and you will live in the glory that will never end." With enthusiasm we accept the invitation and, drawn by the Holy Spirit, we hasten to the font of water that gushes forth eternal life.

The action of entering into church redefines the fruitfulness of the operative action of the Holy Spirit who calls us forth to celebrate the paschal event. A similar movement does not find its origin in the subjects themselves, because in this case the baptized could be tempted to look within themselves, their own expectations and existential perspectives. It is Christ who works in them and who plants the seed in their hearts and the restlessness to see the face of God (cf. Ps 41). The concrete existence is complex and obscure and gives to disciples an intense desire for the light. The hope of rediscovering the light that illuminates and inspires the disciple in the darkness of history is understood in the style of the evangelist, which stimulates all baptized people to place themselves on the road to be in the presence of God in the liturgical assembly and to accept that "spirit of revelation" that guides them to realize the divine will in their everyday lives.

Consequently, in the creative cloud of the divine initiative, disciples place themselves in the position of forgetting about themselves, abandoning all that is not a part of the truth in their lives, in the Spirit go out of the realm of space and time, and immerse themselves in the re-creative action of the three Divine Persons. It is the great event that is present in the liturgical celebration. In a historical/salvific letter, the desire of disciples to accept the invitation of Christ as a condition for celebrating the wonders of God, places them in a condition of exodus, of abandonment, of a way of life animated only by human criteria, to proceed into an experience that illuminates them and regenerates them in the constant rebirth from on high. In their stepping forward into church disciples revive the story of the biblical exodus. This truth is redefined through three signs that accompany them and that qualify their itinerary: the church plaza, the facade of the church, and the door of entrance to the place of assembly.

Overall, the church land represents the incarnation of the history of the world in the experience of the monk who enters the choir by passing through the choir stalls. Here he, in the silence of meditation and in the wonder of his heart, is guided to the liveliness of the faith that intensely "ruminates" the divine history in order to personalize it and to let himself go so he can be filled to the brim with emotion so as to expand his heart as should happen to all believers. In the same way, Christians who go into church listening, meditating, reflecting, and proclaiming the wonders that the Father has planted throughout the history of salvation helps their desire to "go up to the mountain of the Lord" in order to sing the new song to the Highest. The face of Christ portends the whole person of the baptized one who longs to be seated next to the one who is the breath of life, the sense and the behavior of his existence. This process is not activated by any human desires, but it is illuminated by the evangelical annunciation itself, expressed in the architecture and the iconography of the facade of the church. Before the eye of the senses, which brings together the images of salvation history, one's heart is opened to the Spirit because what is always rooted more in the life of every celebrant is the desire to taste how sweet is the Lord. The facade of the place of worship, through its artistic figures and its architectural structure, illuminates that "liturgical desert" that is the church plaza because the walk toward the church is truly full of meaning. Founded on the psalms of ascension (119–27) and the entrance into the temple, the baptized develop a desire to encounter the one who has called them, accompanies them in the Spirit, and offers them the desire to ascend to the fullness of life. A marvelous synthesis is thus revealed in the heart of the believer. In the power of the Holy Spirit, believers hear the invitation of Christ to follow him, they enter in communion with him in the eucharistic celebration, meditating on the history of God with the heart's eye turned toward the face of the church, and, while walking, they feel their hearts increase in the desire to let go in order to encounter in spiritual exultation the one who called them.

The door, then, realizes the Johannine figure of Christ who is the gate for the sheep (cf. John 10:7, 9). The knowledge that only the Lord dead and resurrected can make the Father known stimulates the Christian to live in a more radical way the identification with Christ with the intensity of the Master. The passage from the ordinary story to the liturgical assembly reminds us how its existence is "hidden with Christ in God" (cf. Col 3:3) and how only the full configuration with the paschal experience of the Master allows us to accept in the active and fruitful liturgical participation with our brothers and sisters in the faith. The words of Jesus in the conviviality of the Last Supper are remembered: "I am the way, and the truth, and the life. No one comes to the Father except through me" (John 14:6). This truth stimulates us to live out the action of crossing the threshold as a positive, significant decision in one's personal existence. Thus, only in Christ celebrated in the fraternal communion are people able to uncover their own existence, live, and make more meaningful the beauty of existence. Christians know that only in the encounter with God made man, present in the hall of the liturgical assembly, will they be able to participate in that light that never sets and that will guide them on the pathway of time, while waiting for the ultimate fullness of glory.

29

Exiting the Church

The liturgical celebration offers the Christian community the possibility to enter into God's repose, to illuminate history for all eternity, to regenerate the human creature in its personal identity. The sacramental action helps the disciples enjoy the gift of revealing themselves in the presence of God and allows them to mature in the experience of salvation.

The leaving of the assembly assigns to the disciples of the Lord the task of seminating in human history the faith, the hope, and the charity to celebrate and share in the divine mysteries. The Roman Missal tells us that the assembly is dismissed so that "each may go out to do good works, praising and blessing God" (*General Instruction of the Roman Missal* 90). Such an indication ritually assumes the experience that the Risen shared with his own when he appeared to them the morning of Easter: "Peace be with you. As the Father has sent me, so I send you" (John 20:21). That which the evangelist offers us in his narrative of the apparitions of the risen Lord is always present and operative in the liturgical assembly that hears again the call to the mission that the Master gave to his disciples. When the reunited assembly hears the invitation of the ordained minister, "Go in the peace of Christ," and in the exultation for the divine wonders it responds, "Thanks be to God," it is invested in this vocation. In this final dialogue, in fact, the baptized have the admonition in the significance of leaving the place of worship to go out and enter into the space-time of humanity in order to testify the newness that the risen Lord has brought to the world, to seminate hope that comes from God, to offer their own lives in historical martyrdom, to proclaim to the world that Christ has made all things new, and to share with their brothers and sisters the tension as they move toward the eternal Pasch in heaven.

In the celebration, the glorified Christ has offered us the elements to construct in truth one's existence, the Holy Spirit has enfolded us with his inebriating embrace, and the communion with the brothers and sisters has invited us to work in history with the passion of one who wishes to build a true path of openness to all the world in order to initiate an authentic experience of fraternity according to the eternal design of the Father. That which is celebrated in the ritual is destined to qualify one's everyday journey. In fact, there exists a close relationship between that which is celebrated in mystery and that which must be incarnated on a daily basis. If approaching the temple was given life by the believing acceptance of the Master and the celebration has significance for the disciples of being transformed by his love, then exiting the church represents the need to build a life in light of Christ's Pasch. The ordinary nature of life represents the real place for existential creativity of the disciples of the Lord. The disciples feel called to meditate in their daily choices on the paschal love of the three persons of the Most Holy Trinity, which are the historical contingencies of each day. Thus, from the disciples' existence can truly flow the cosmic hymn to the Father through Christ and in the Holy Spirit. This journey is possible only because they have enjoyed sacramentally the divine fullness. Through such a participative dynamic in the rite they have been wrapped up in the fullness of trinitarian love, they have enjoyed the fulfillment of the divine promises, they have been re-created by the power of the Holy Spirit, and they feel energized to assume always in a more lively way the mentality of the Master. Such richness is truly realized when an exuberance in communication of the mystery with one's brothers and sisters develops. They reach out in the desire to realize their own existence. The liturgical celebration constitutes a prophetic sign for all humanity, which continually seeks meaning for its own existence.

The church plaza, then, becomes the space of renewed Pentecost for the Christian community, which proclaims the wonders of God and becomes the opportune occasion to touch all people who in the walk of history find themselves thirsty for the truth, seeking the font that satiates their drought. Christians, who descend from the liturgy into daily life, become a hymn to the beauty of life, and this testimonial attitude must fascinate the brothers and sisters, who are able to rediscover in them a guide to find the light "which enlightens everyone, was coming into the world" (John 1:9).

There are three possible works that the risen Lord asks of one who has been regenerated in his love: the work of developing communion, the operative knowledge of the temporary nature of human history, and the difficulty of achieving the fullness of life.

The liturgical assembly, when it comes together, enjoys everything, just as in the experience of celebrated faith people find the truth of their vocation: to build up the history of humanity as a real story of fraternity in the image of communion that exists in the Most Holy Trinity. The eucharistic communion is at the same time the point of departure and the point of arrival for this project, which should define the hopes and decisions of everyday life.

In the context of the liturgical assembly, the heart of the faithful is open to the universality of the gift of salvation, through the rite that they have brought within all humanity in an inexpressible spiritual attraction in Christ Jesus. This experience is redefined in living relationships with authenticity and oneness with every person, whatever the situation, because they realize the meaning of the universal communion for which Jesus gave his life. At the same time, the knowledge of the temporary nature of the liturgical celebration stimulates the disciple to work in history with the spirituality of a passerby who intensely lives in the moment, knowing, however, that this is not the end but the middle of life. Christians entering into history are not afraid of living in conformity with the Gospel, of incarnating their mentality to that of the Master, of reading and loving history with their own love, because the meaning of life is so much greater. People who in the sacramental celebration accept the gift of the fullness of divine love, enjoy in their own hearts the freedom of Christ and do not allow themselves to be prisoners of their situations in life. Freed by Christ in the Spirit, the baptized live the gift of freedom in the daily decisions of life, allowing themselves to be crucified by the world's culture in order to seminate the joy that comes from on high in the hearts of their brothers and sisters.

The concrete work of reflection enlivens the community to orient itself toward the fullness of glory and the fulfillment of every desire. The liturgical celebration places itself in an eternal blessed dimension and is oriented in a fruitful waiting while reflecting the fullness of divine love. This awaiting the heavenly Jerusalem stimulates the community to share the lordship of Christ in becoming part of the events of history, enjoying the access to the Garden of Eden, and drawing near to the tree of life.

This analysis helps us to understand the rite of the dismissal of the assembly, not as a conclusion of a formal and juridical action, but as a point of departure to go out and build up the world in the enthusiasm of the Spirit, according to the model "seen" in the celebration of the divine mysteries, and to give to the world conceived by the Father a place of communion through daily work within the framework of the final realization of the kingdom. When they exit the church, Christians enter into the roads of history, spreading out the fruitfulness of the rule of Christ and the enthusiasm of the Spirit, in an inexhaustible procession of freedom, in a way that every human creature desires, in anticipation of their own full and total transfiguration in the beauty of the vision of the three Divine Persons, full completion of the history of all humanity.

30

Dipping

Upon entering church Christians dip their hands in the holy water and trace the sign of the cross on themselves. It is through this action that the significance of their entrance into the edifice is understood: to renew the knowledge of their baptismal vocation by entering into the church community in order to celebrate the divine mysteries. With their baptism, they have become the recipients of the free love of God, which, in Christ, has regenerated them, and in the ecclesial celebration they sing praise for the mercy of the Father and understand themselves as sinful creatures made new constantly by the Holy Spirit. For this reason it is important to have baptismal fonts at the doors of the church so that the truth of the gift of rebirth by water and the Spirit is always made present in the evangelical mind of every baptized person. The joy of the liturgical assembly in entering and contemplating the risen Lord comes from the renewed understanding of its baptismal vocation to be a new creature in Christ. Overall, it is important to understand the significance of the holy water in regard to this. It is particularly interesting to read the promises in the ritual: "On the basis of age-old custom, water is one of the signs that the Church often uses in blessing the faithful. Holy water reminds the faithful of Christ, who is given to us as the supreme divine blessing, who called himself the living water, and who in water established baptism for our sake as the sacramental sign of the blessing that brings salvation" (*Book of Blessings* 1388).

Water possesses in itself a deep existential value, since in its intense significance it reinterprets the meaning of everyday life. The image that it presents to us is very edifying. The human being cannot live without drinking water; it is a question of life and death. This profound truth constitutes the starting point of its use in human language. The action of immersing oneself in water gives new meaning to the human desire to return to the font of life and come forth from it reborn. Only in this way does a person have the possibility of going forth with renewed spirit into the complex and varied pathways in life. From this perspective we understand why people, when they want to understand their inner selves and try to understand the true meaning of life, become aware of an intense thirst for the truth and quench it from the font that is able to restore and illuminate them and that, from the obscurity of history, fills them with hope. This figurative dimension takes place in the baptismal regeneration. The journey that gives the acquired faith its dynamic character through the image of thirst shows human beings that they cannot exist without choosing faith, at the risk of destroying one's old self. Upon reflection, persons who accept the gift of regeneration in water and the Holy Spirit accept the new existence that deepens their thirst and brings them closer to the font of living water that is Christ. This is the experience of the Samaritan woman in the Gospel of John (John 4). The Holy Spirit, in fact, generates in baptism an inexhaustible thirst for Christ and gives that gift in the celebration of the divine mysteries. In a certain way, all believers relive in their person the experience of the psalmist, who re-interprets the longing to rest in God through the imagery of thirst (Ps 42) or of the "dry and weary land where there is no water" (Ps 63:1). In the action of entering the church, Christians show the desire to abandon the weariness of everyday life and relive their own sacramental initiation in Christ, which represents a constant journey of maturation in the newness of evangelical life (cf. Rom 6:4). In the action of dipping the hand into the holy water, believers express the desire to become regenerated by the Spirit and to deepen, within the ecclesiastical community, the existential significance of choosing Christ, which first took place the day of their baptism. In fact, the fruitfulness of the celebration of the divine mysteries is tied to the lively waiting for the sacramental encounter with the Lord, source of living water. The drama of baptism would emerge in all of its truth if they would enter into the sacramental encounter with the Lord without coveting the mystery with all of their person. The gesture of dipping the hand in holy water gives life to this spiritual situation, which should be a constant in one's spiritual life.

The sign of the cross identifies the meaning of this thirst: the paschal event of the Master. If it is true that every person lives an intense longing for the true meaning of life, disciples of the Lord in particular always have their gaze turned toward Christ, dead and risen, since only in turning from one's own destiny and introspection is one able to appreciate the light that comes from on high. The action of dipping the hand in holy water, accompanied by the sign of the cross, proclaims a life of self-denial in order to enter more deeply into the celebration of the paschal mysteries: to expand the thirst of absorbing the paschal event since only here can the thirst of life be sated and can one effectively rediscover the truth of one's existence. Thus within the structure of the ritual a relationship develops between dipping the hand in holy water and the placing of the fragment of the consecrated host into the chalice filled with wine and the distribution of the eucharistic gifts through the signs of bread and wine. The action of dipping the hand into holy water celebrates the divine mysteries in the body of Christ who is the church. This experience of communion is understood in the eucharistic body, which is expressed in the sign of consecrated bread. Contemplating Christ who presides over the eucharistic celebration, baptized persons are warned that they cannot have the evangelical experience of communion without imitating the sacrifice of Christ. By saying "Amen" before the bread dipped into the wine, Christians witness their faith in the truth of the communion in the one body of Christ by sharing in his blood. Thus life in the church is realized only if one is willing to continuously live the desire to freely give one's own blood. This is the path that is therefore given to whomever desires to be a disciple of Christ.

Baptism, seen again in the action of personal faith and within the path of the church, is fully realized in the Eucharist in which Christ gives to every disciple the full realization of the promises made by the Master: "Let anyone who is thirsty come to me" (John 7:37), and "Whoever comes to me will never be hungry, and whoever believes in me will never be thirsty" (John 6:35). Whoever immerses themselves in Christ dead and risen through their baptismal faith is quenched in his blood and inhales trinitarian communion.

In this context, which gives life to the eucharistic celebration, Christians draw near to the banquet of the kingdom, where the Holy Spirit gives real food and drink; consequently, Christ fills them with the messianic gifts (cf. Isa 55:1-2), and offers them the possibility of drawing near in the eucharistic prayer to the presence of the Father, contemplative fulfillment in the true meaning of life.

In the rite that takes place at the holy water fonts at the entrance of church all disciples of the Lord proclaim their faith in the paschal mystery. They proclaim in the ritual action their desire to live every moment in the eternal light and to live by the Spirit in order to enjoy

95

in the sacramental events the beauty and fruitfulness of life in the church, which, while awaiting the heavenly Jerusalem, is where he will always be able to drink from the "the river of the water of life, bright as crystal, flowing from the throne of God and of the Lamb" (Rev 22:1).

31

Fasting

One particular gesture that the church offers us during the season of Lent is fasting, which in the depth of the liturgical experience becomes a sacramental event: one relives the life of the Master in his own fast of forty days in the desert (cf. preface of the first Sunday of Lent). Such an action is of highest relevance, since it presupposes an ongoing closeness with Christ in order to share the paschal event of his death, burial, and resurrection with him (cf. 1 Cor 15:3-4). One's ascetic aspiration redefines an intense contemplative experience. In fact, the fruitful truth of every journey is based on the solid foundation of contemplation of the face of Christ. The language of fasting reinterprets the interior communion with Jesus dead and resurrected (cf. *Sacrosanctum Concilium* 110) in order to enjoy the resurrection in the fullness of the paschal event. The prayer of the blessing of the ashes is very meaningful "through the spiritual journey of Lent, (your children) arrive completely renewed to the celebration of the Pasch of your Son, Christ our Lord."

First of all, it is important to always remember that the truth of every expression in the journey of the praying Christian community presupposes a noncommunal spiritual experience. To set aside natural food is itself a profession of faith in the lordship of Christ in the heart of the disciple; it is "to sing existentially" the primacy of the Absolute. Christians have the gaze of their hearts fixated on the Master; it is the same vocation of any disciple. The experience of fasting, which invests the whole person of all believers and that of the whole Christian community, redefines their prayerful desire that the Lord make himself present in their lives, illuminate their decisions, and fill them with the newness of the paschal mystery. The season of Lent represents a particularly significant time from this point of view; it is the prophecy of the ascetic drive that should accompany the disciple of the Lord in the daily work of baptismal conversion. It is, therefore, by its nature a catechumenal time during which one deepens the experience of being a disciple who cannot live without knowing one's radical poverty and being given divine mercy. Such interior action draws the attention of the person completely toward Christ and offers, as a spontaneous consequence, the forgetting of immediate needs of the human creature. The experience of faith requires the ability to leave the sphere of the "I," to forget oneself in order to rediscover oneself, to recuperate the joy of one's existence, to underline the interior enthusiasm in light of the running of daily life. The fascination of beauty is thus brought together into the ordinary context of faith. Here people enjoy forgetting about themselves so as not to lose the full contemplation of that which draws them in and offers them the full pleasure of life. We see in this context then how the experience of fasting represents a profession of faith of the Christian community that proclaims the lordship of the Master in its life.

Thus the fact that fasting is tied to the sign of not eating allows us to appreciate more fully its theological significance. All creatures in their actual journey need nutrition in order to exist and develop relationships with their brothers and sisters. This necessity is primordial for existence. The choice then of fasting elevates to the primary position the one who is true and eternal food for every person. In choosing to fast, the baptized place themselves on a higher plane. Their nutrient is Christ in the mystery of the incarnate Word, dead and risen, the one who, in relationship with them, gives true realization to their personhood, just as the Father has done from all eternity. In such a way the renunciation of material food becomes an efficacious sign of the desire for heavenly food: to be seated at the banquet of the eternal communion with the three Divine Persons, and with them, to live with all of their brothers and sisters in the light of the heavenly Jerusalem.

The liturgy then associates the experience of fasting with the imposition of ashes, with an interesting theological/spiritual interpretation. The Lenten process takes the baptized to "new life in Christ," as the prayer of the church still teaches us. This goal is possible if the old person, through penitential ascension into the life-giving contemplation of Christ, destroys the exterior person in order that the new person created in the image and likeness of God be reborn from the dust. Thus this person is a living participant to the glory of the risen Lord. The experience of fasting incarnates the paschal sense of existence for every disciple, called to die in and with the death of Jesus in order to rise in and with him at the resurrection. This vitality allows us to see in a positive light the penitential action of disciples, since the principle that defines their new existence is nothing other than the rising with Christ toward the final glorious communion with the Father, allowing themselves in his emptiness to arrive at death on the cross. By fasting, the baptized longs to grow in the freedom of Christ in order to rise always higher into the mystery of life, as fruitful participation in the trinitarian communion. The baptized long to breathe the divine breath, celebrating the primacy of Christ and the creativity of the Spirit in order to make of themselves a simple and essential glorification of the Father. Fasting stimulates all disciples to love themselves in the divine now, in which they long to be formed by the Spirit in order to be a transparent reflection of the brilliant countenance of Christ.

This is not confined to the baptized person, but becomes fruitful in the construction of future relationships. Fasting brings the disciple of the Lord to a progressive openness to the other, to assume the dynamics and problems of everyday life, for the creation of a journey of effective solidarity, whether with regard to spiritual experiences or for material needs. The gift of the Holy Spirit, which takes the journey of fasting in imitation of the action of Jesus, enables the baptized to engage in interpersonal relationships in order to build an authentic fraternal communion. The Christian, in fact, knows that the understanding of any decision or of any attitude that wants to effectively be evangelical must constantly be oriented toward the communal life. It is to this end that every believer's action is based. The point of reference is the eucharistic celebration. The eucharistic mystery gives meaning to fasting, which represents the font and the culmination of every penitential experience that wishes to be truly evangelical. It is in the Eucharist that the church rediscovers its very truth and being.

The tradition of the church has indicated to the Christian community the need to live the condition of fasting before it can draw near to the true and full participation of the eucharistic mystery. Such orientation is outside of every possible juridical or moral law, but reinterprets the believer's knowledge that all baptized people, when they present themselves before the Lord, must have a pure heart, a heart free and freed, an open and docile heart so that the Master can implant his word, form them in the Holy Spirit, and feed them with his body and with his blood. The truth of the sacramental celebration is formed in people with attentive and open hearts who are animated by the believing supplication in such a way that the Lord of life appears on the horizon, making his home in them and regenerating them on a path of constant newness of life. Thus the baptized person, leaving behind incidental realities, matures in those realities that are eternal and enjoys, in the liturgical assembly, communion with the three Divine Persons.

This process will inevitably make flourish the experience of ecclesiastical and universal communion, which qualifies the Eucharist as such and which in itself is continually renewed. In Christ Jesus exists all of humanity, and every action that is qualified by the Eucharist must be a clear reflection of him. The truth of one's baptismal vocation to conversion in the language of fasting is reinterpreted in the development of thirst for fraternal communion, according to the apostolic ideal (cf. Acts 2:44-45; 4:32-35). Only in this way is the church able to become a prophecy before the whole world of a new humanity.

32

Kissing

One type of language that we find in liturgical tradition, but uniquely in popular piety, is the use of the kiss as a ritual-effective experience. This gesture, already used in the sign of peace, is felt particularly by the religious person to express the desire of communion with the transcendent. In this gesture the existence of the human is incarnated in the "nutrition" by the divine, in order to have an existential security while going through the obscure and problematic path of daily life. A similar action, very significant in popular piety, finds its "evangelical" roots, when we consider the gestures of the sacramental celebration.

In the liturgical perspective the parameter of reference is the rite of the adoration of the cross in the liturgical action of Good Friday. The ritual dynamic here guides us in understanding the significance of the kiss in celebrative language. At the presentation of the mystery of the cross, "This is the wood of the cross, on which hung the Savior of the world," the assembly acclaims, "Come, let us worship."

In this celebrative dialogue, we intuit how the reception of the gifts of salvation come to us through contemplation of the object of faith: Christ the Pasch, who gives himself to hungry and thirsty humanity, the gift of salvation. In this relationship, the word "adoration" constitutes the key element. If we search deeper into the meaning of "adoration" we discover how this term reinterprets the interpersonal rapport that is established with the kiss: to effectively be mouth to mouth. Adoration is therefore a rapport of relational intimacy, where one intentionally lives in the other person, in an "inexhaustible feast to expand the greatness of reciprocity." Thus emerges the understanding of being able to possess the gift that others make of themselves for the building up of an intimate reciprocity that progressively brings existential fusion of two persons.

Kissing the crucifix in the liturgical action of Good Friday is not a "pietistic" gesture, which would be limited to a simple emotional context, but it holds the true significance of the Christian choice: the vocation to identify oneself with the feelings of the Crucified. Through the sign of the kiss of the crucifix Christians express the believers' desire to abandon themselves so as to become involved in their own paschal identities. In that kiss of the crucifix, Christians express their will to base every daily choice in the effective and affective communion with that event of salvation. The same itinerary of faith, illuminated by the word of God, always builds up more in the disciple the search for personal identity. Therefore, it is in the Master that people go outside of their historical solitude and allow themselves to be regenerated by the relationship that the paschal announcement of the crucifix is able to offer them. It is the image of "eating the Word" in the prophets and the book of Revelation. The desire of the communion of believers becomes an action, and in the action the creatures incarnate their desire for communion and they feel encouraged, in a constant tension with the inexhaustible transfiguring relationship with Christ dead and risen. A similar prospective has, then, its fulfillment at the moment of the eucharistic communion, which represents the ultimate part of the liturgical action of Good Friday. The "eating of the word" in the kiss becomes the "sacramental eating of the body and the blood of the Lord" in communion. Here people live in a unique way the reciprocity with the risen Lord who brings within himself the signs of the passion; here they feed that hope that is consolation in the emptiness and dryness of life. Here is given the foretaste of the eternal banquet in Revelation (22:14), in the image of the kiss in the Song of Songs (1:1), recaptured in the mystagogical catechesis of St. Ambrose.

This action, which the Christian community lives on Good Friday, is reinterpreted in eucharistic adoration, where one lives in faith the desire for communion with Christ. Eating with the mouth, an expression that begins with the action of the kiss, becomes an eating with the eyes of faith. The heart of the disciple, which feels attracted to the Master in order to become smaller in his presence, with the eyes of the loved one "eats" his Lord with the "kiss of the heart." This action reveals how the gesture of kissing incarnates the need present in all people to establish a true and fruitful reciprocity with the Lord, font and sense of their existence. In such a way the action of kissing purifies one from every psychological sensitivity, reinterprets ritually a living profession of faith, and becomes the manifestation of the spiritual life for whoever walks in the unconditional following of the divine Master.

Whoever attends a school of liturgy is aided in being able to understand the desire of the religious person to kiss sacred objects, such as the images of saints, reliquaries, statues, and objects that have some connection with the world of the sacred. A celebrative element that can help us live such actions of faith is the kiss of the altar, which the ministers give at the beginning of the celebration. This action explains the veneration of the centrality of the altar, figure of Christ, altar-priest-victim of the sacrifice itself, as well as the intense desire to share the oblative dimension of Christ. The presence of the relics of the martyrs under the altar adds "the communion in the one sacrifice of the whole Church of Christ, with which it confesses and testifies, if necessary also with blood, the faithfulness of his spouse and Lord" (rite of the dedication of a church and altar).

Christians are a living sacrifice in Christ, holy and pleasing to God, and their "devotional" kiss incarnates the oblative dimension of faith. This vision gives believing fruitfulness to every religious experience, which gives a kiss.

In the fulfillment of such ritual, humanity has the sensation of truly entering into contact with the divine and nearly of possessing God in a way that brings a security in the daily path of everyday life. Religious persons are always tempted to approach the divine in order to enslave God to their own projects, to their own desires, and to their own expectations. The sense of the divine is very strong in the heart of humans and that determines ritual actions; a person's sensibility finds gratification in the search for a relationship with God. Also, if in certain manifestations one has the sensation of dynamics that are outside of normal logic, the anxiety that the divine would enter into the religious person determines one's actions. In these mechanisms the oral dimension is that which perhaps best allows them to perceive this contact/possession. In such a way they have the intense sensation that the divine penetrates into their person and refreshes them in the problems of everyday life. The result is surely momentary and unfortunately precarious for psychological peace of mind.

In front of these instinctive languages of the religious person, the believer must begin a process of purification. The rediscovery of the value of the corporeality of the daily culture helps one to see the significance of the devotional gesture of the kiss. Baptized persons must illuminate the affective intentionality of their heart, which in the charm of Christ longs to be possessed by him in a journey of inexhaustible divine-human reciprocity. In fact, the evangelical element that permits us to overcome possible devotional or magical dimensions is the constant search for the motivations of the one who gives the gesture of the kiss. We must interpret that which, at first impression, could result instinctively in the profession of faith for the person who accepts with pureness of heart the graciousness of God through the kiss of the image, in order to rediscover the hope that comes from on high and the serene and courageous docility it gives to incarnate the mysterious presence of the Lord of life.

Conclusion

In its instructions regarding the reform of the liturgy, Vatican II stimulated the Christian community to move toward the rediscovery of the mystery hidden for centuries in God and revealed to it in Christ Jesus by means of signs. The understanding of the language of the liturgy is important so that the faithful may reach toward this offer of salvation, which the Father has extended them in Christ Jesus and in the Holy Spirit.

As disciples of the Lord we live with the Invisible, and we are enthralled by his mystery of death and resurrection. We desire to walk with the Master toward Jerusalem in order to be associated definitively with his glory. We are guided by the Spirit to the Father, and we long for eternal life with the Father, the Son, and the Holy Spirit.

The divine power that allows us to enact the liturgical signs with spiritual fruitfulness and richness involves us in the mystery present in those signs. It makes us ascend with Jesus toward Jerusalem in order to stand always in the presence of the Father, contemplating God's glory. It permits us to give flesh to the richness of love that defines our heart and our desires each day. It offers us the joy of making our own the ritual actions that are the short steps to reach the full stature of Christ.

An understanding of the actions that define the sacraments should help lead us to eternal life. The various rituals speak of the power of faith, of the joy of belonging to Christ, of a desire to taste the mystery by forgetting ourselves, of a longing to sing of the true meaning of life, and of an anxiousness to grow in the richness of this eternal relationship.

The richness of the liturgy is not, however, cut off from the daily journey of the community. It is based in the ordinariness of life and retraces itself in it. Through these signs Jesus Christ places us in an ineffable relationship of love with the Father and with himself, so that by means of the small and simple gestural actions of our lives we may develop the greatness of God's love offered to us in the great event of the sacramental celebration.

The truth of the liturgical celebration is found in everyday life where we proclaim with our whole being the complete lordship of Christ and where we grow in the expectation of the full manifestation of his glory. The sign of his giving to us the Invisible presents itself each day, helping us move toward the moment of passing from earthly life to eternity.

Therefore the effort to profoundly read the value of the ritual actions that we repeat with a certain frequency should help us to overcome the easy temptation of ritualistic habit and to see, upon reflection, the wonderful divine communication with us.

This sign, lived in faith, represents our prayer to the Father, so that the Father may help the Christian community to long for the communion that awaits us in the kingdom. Communion with our brothers and sisters in eternal praise will be the fulfillment of the richness of the sacramental celebrations.

Our regular and prayerful participation in the liturgy helps us address our concerns and give thanks to God.

To live the signs of the liturgy means to incarnate our own faith, rich with prayer, in these words and actions and to rejoice in the certainty of the Father's presence and the paschal mystery of Christ.